D0467892

SAN MATEO LIBRARY

DISCARDED

THE GENIUS OF THE
GREEK DRAMA

THE GENIUS OF THE GREEK DRAMA

GREEK DRAMA

Three Plays

being the *Agamemnon* of Aeschylus
the *Antigone* of Sophocles & the
Medea of Euripides rendered and
adapted with an Introduction

by

CYRIL E. ROBINSON

Play Anthology Reprint Series

 BOOKS FOR LIBRARIES PRESS
FREEPORT, NEW YORK

LIBRARY
COLLEGE OF SAN MATEO

First Published 1921

Reprinted 1970 by arrangement with Oxford University Press, Inc.

GREAT THEATRE ATHENS

INTERNATIONAL STANDARD BOOK NUMBER:
0-8369-8217-7

LIBRARY OF CONGRESS CATALOG CARD NUMBER:
70-132138

PRINTED IN THE UNITED STATES OF AMERICA

98757

PREFACE

TO reproduce in English words the true spirit of an ancient masterpiece is admittedly impossible. To curtail or alter it appears an impudence. And for the twofold presumption, of which I am here guilty, some words of explanation and apology seem due.

The reading of plays is nowadays a common pastime with both old and young, and more especially the reading of plays aloud. The dramatic literature of England, suitable to the class-room or the study circle, is, however, soon exhausted; and for that reason, if no other, the literature of Greece will find a vogue. Now, Greek plays are not like English. The study of *Hamlet* or of *Julius Caesar* may without great loss be interrupted and resumed; but the artistic unity of a Greek play is so pronounced and so much the most essential of its qualities that to break the thread is ruinous. The whole is more vital than the parts. It should be read at a sitting. In the renderings here given I have therefore aimed at bringing each play within the compass of one hour's recitation. Much of the original has been omitted; but the contraction is less damaging than might be supposed. The final scenes, which, I think, have suffered most, are not of such consequence as in a play of Shakespeare; for the Greek poets favoured a somewhat long and slow declension from the climax to the close, which is against our modern taste. Similarly, the Choric Interludes, which have suffered some foreshortening, are without direct bearing on the structure of the plot. The bulk of the Dialogue remains.

I have kept another possibility in view. The revival of amateur theatrical production is on the increase; and here, too, the Classic Drama may serve a useful part. The contraction of the plays is for this purpose no serious disadvantage. On the contrary, for girls and boys at any rate, a play which numbers seven hundred lines is much more manageable than a play of twice that length. So in the Introduction I have tried to indicate the lines on which such presentation might be planned; and in the rendering of the text I have even admitted a few such alterations as may facilitate and simplify the task. The main characters are few; which is no drawback. The numbers of the Chorus may be expanded or diminished at discretion; and the problem of scenic decoration is here remarkably straightforward. In short, the staging of a Classic Drama should present attractions, which, I hope, may lead to more numerous attempts than hitherto. They will repay.

INTRODUCTION

I. The Authors.

IN the year 480 before Christ the great Armada of Xerxes, King of Persia, fought and was destroyed in the straits of Salamis within full view of the Citadel of Athens. In that resounding victory, whereby the destinies of Greece were saved, Aeschylus the soldier-poet played his part, being numbered very possibly (if we may guess from the peculiarly vivid detail of his own description of the scene *) among that party of Greek men-at-arms who were ferried across the strait to a small island in mid-channel, there to butcher in cold blood a marooned detachment of the Persian host.

In the celebrations which followed on the victory, Sophocles, thus early an adept in the art to which he was always particularly partial, took his place (so legend says) among the dancing band of choir-boys.

In that year Euripides was born.

A quarter of a century elapsed; and then, in 456, Aeschylus died. The time of his death marked, by a strangely appropriate coincidence, an era in the history of his country. Athens, hitherto the champion of Greek liberties, declared herself definitely about this very date the imperial mistress of the league of free Hellenic states which had been formed to withstand the Persians, but which by this high-handed act of hers became no longer free. Thus Athens stood forth confessed as a tyrant city. It was a turning-point in her destiny; and a turning-point in more senses than one. Pericles, the great statesman who led and directed the new imperialist policy, was an enthusiastic lover of the arts. In his own words, he aimed at making Athens the intellectual ' school-mistress ' of Greece,

* In his play, *The Persian Men.*

no less than her political mistress. To this end he endeavoured to attract to Athens all the best wits and artists of the Greek world. The town became a centre of culture, and, it is not too much to say, the birth-place of a new learning. For along with the artists and poets there came to Athens many philosophers and thinkers—'Sophists', they called themselves—who preached strange new-fangled doctrines about God and man. These men looked at the world from an angle hitherto unknown. They had discovered—as the men in the Renaissance of the sixteenth century re-discovered—that much of the old tradition and many of the old religious beliefs were no longer tenable. They discarded the old view that a man's prime duty was complete subservience to the established order of the State. They expressed the then startling theory that a man must think for himself, act for himself, and even formulate and test for himself the foundations of religious belief. They taught men, in short, to be Individuals first, and Citizens afterwards. In the two brilliant generations of artistic and intellectual output which followed, most of the plays of Sophocles and Euripides were written.

So passed another half-century, and Athens stood again at the cross-roads. She had gone to war with her great Peloponnesian rival, Sparta ; the war had lasted for over twenty years and was now drawing to its weary close. In 406 Athens threw away her last opportunity of making a safe and honourable peace. In that year Sophocles and Euripides both died. Two summers later Athens herself had fallen, and lay at the mercy of her Spartan conquerors.

Between the old order of the days of the Persian Invasion and the new Athens of the Sophist movement and the Peloponnesian war there was, spiritually at least, a great gulf fixed. The old ideal had been a conservative and narrowly patriotic ideal. The new Athens stood for progress, freedom of thought and freedom of conscience ; and was liberal in all else except the policy which rendered the maintenance of her empire a necessity to her safe existence. Now in a very real sense Aeschylus and Euripides were, each in his own way, typical of the two conflicting schools of thought. Aeschylus was a man of the old school, who believed supremely in the State and who at the climax of his life had risked his person for her in battle against the 'long-haired Medes'. That fact was recorded to the exclusion of all else upon his tombstone : and it is symbolic of the man. He upheld the tradition of his forefathers, and was before everything a patriotic and loyal citizen of the State. The Athenians themselves regarded him as a sort of major prophet, the prop and pillar of the old conservatism and of the orthodox religious creed. It is true that so profound a mind as his could not wholly escape those obstinate questionings and inward doubts concerning the deep mysteries of life which must naturally vex the soul of every great philosopher or poet. But he dealt with those problems in the pious and humble spirit of the author of the Book of Job. He never came out in revolt against orthodox opinion ; and when, half a century after his death and on the very eve of her final catastrophe, Aristophanes the comic playwright wished to denounce the evil courses of the sophist-ridden town, he turned back inevitably to the grand old poet of his country's prime. In his comedy the *Frogs* he brought back, as it were, to life, and confronted in wordy dialogue upon the stage, Euripides the 'seducer' and Aeschylus the 'saviour' of Athens.

The Prodigal Son is always a more arresting personality than the more staid and well-behaved brother who waited at home ; and Euripides the rebel has a charm for us which the orthodox Aeschylus lacks. Individualist as he was, Euripides' whole interest lay in the workings of the human character and mind. The old myths appealed to him only as providing material for the study of man and of the problems of life. Like Dickens, he shocked his contemporaries by the realism with which he portrayed individuals of the lower orders—the slave, the family nurse, or the 'pedagogue'. In the *Medea* he has bent himself to master and understand the psychology of the wronged wife and the tragedy of the broken home. Living in an age which regarded woman as her husband's chattel, he suddenly threw upon the life of the downtrodden sex all the brilliant illumination of his keen sympathy and insight. His enemies pretended that he was a misogynist, because his heroines displayed the frailties of their nature; but, in reality, he was the first of the ancients to appreciate and understand woman. He was ahead of his time; and, as is so frequently the fate of pioneers, his genius won him little but abuse. During his life he was almost continuously unpopular. At the time of his death he was in exile at a foreign prince's court; and it was only when a new generation arose that his plays were valued at their true worth. During the succeeding century they were acted over and over again not merely at Athens but in the outlying colonies of Greece, and posterity, more especially in modern times, has felt a peculiar sense of spiritual kinship with Euripides 'the Human'.

The genius of Sophocles, standing midway between his rivals in point of actual time, represents also a kind of mean between their literary qualities. He was not a prophet like Aeschylus; nor a philosopher like Euripides. Rather, he was an artist pure and simple, and an artist of a peculiarly Greek stamp. 'Nothing too much' was the legend inscribed above the temple front at Delphi; and it might well have been taken as the motto of Sophocles himself. He does not rant, as Aeschylus was often accused of doing. He allows himself no undue excess of passion or emotion such as Euripides not infrequently displays. He sticks like a good artist to a middle course; and seldom rises above, never drops below, an even level of masterly but restrained craftsmanship. As we may guess from this, he was no realist. His characters, like the statues of his contemporary Pheidias, were idealizations or types rather than close studies from the life. So, whereas Aeschylus depicted human beings on a heroic godlike scale, such as they never could have been, while Euripides depicted them as they actually were, Sophocles preferred (as he is himself reported to have said) to draw men and women ' as they should be drawn '.

The style reflects the man; and in style no less than in character there is a wide and striking difference between the three dramatists. Aeschylus thunders in the grand style, which was appropriate to a prophet of patriotism, but which his critics often stigmatized as bombast. He abounds in high-flown passages; he piles on the colour with a lordly hand; he coins new words at will to suit his fancy, words compounded of nouns, verbs, and adjectives strung together in resounding polysyllables, words, as Aristophanes jestingly remarks, with ' shaggy crests ' and ' beetling brows '. Yet the sweep and majesty of his lines is irresistible, and the wealth of imagery, metaphor, and figure displays for a Greek an almost oriental exuberance. It is a style fitted to the heroes and demigods in whose mouths the lines were set. Sophocles is more restrained —a complete master of words and a flawless artist in his use of them; but he cannot rise to the same heights of fancy as his older rival. His poetry is to that of Aeschylus as the chiselled delicacy of the Ionic temple beside the rugged grandeur of the Doric. In comparison with these two, Euripides is apt at first sight to seem commonplace. Often his lines are little above the level of good prose: but he, too, had his peculiar merits. The child of an age which delighted in sophistical argument and political debate, he excels in the thrust and parry of quick dialogue, in the quibbling subtleties of apt retort, in the close-packed logic of a telling speech in which phrase by phrase the point is remorselessly thrust home. There is, too, more light and shade in Euripides than in any other of the ancients. In the development of his characters he plays upon the whole gamut of feeling and passion; and Medea pursues the path to her revenge not with the uniform ferocity and determination of a Clytamnestra, but with the more human diversity of moods such as we find in a Hamlet or a Macbeth, passing through a series of emotional storms and varying between the savage indignation of a jilted wife and the pathetic tenderness of a mother's love. One may guess that Euripides could make an audience feel miserable. That perhaps is one reason why during his lifetime he won such scanty triumphs in his art, and why of the first prizes which were bestowed upon successful dramatists, and of which Sophocles won twenty and Aeschylus fifteen, Euripides received but five.

II. GREEK TRAGEDY.

Having thus far insisted upon the points of difference between the three great dramatists, it is high time we turned to their points of similarity. Tradition and fidelity to convention was the pith and soul of Greek art. The master artist of one genera- tion, whether sculptor, architect, or poet, was imitated by his pupil of the next with an almost slavish adherence ; and even when the pupil felt it in him to go beyond his master, it was only to improve and amplify upon the same old theme. Hence artistic development was continuous. There were no futurists at Athens. This may even be observed in points of minute detail. Thus, for example, Cassandra in the *Agamemnon* compares Clytamnestra to the fabulous monster Scylla ; and Euripides, wishing to supply a suitable figure of abuse for Medea, falls back upon the same comparison. Or again, the Messenger's remarks in the Medea upon the vanity of human life bear a strong resemblance to the Guard's prefatory speech when he comes to announce the death of Antigone. But on much wider lines than these there were accepted conven- tions and canons of Greek Tragedy : and first, in the main theme of Tragedy itself. It must be remembered that the plays were in essence part of a religious ceremony like the

Mystery plays of mediaeval England. Every year in spring, when the festival of the Great Dionysia was held, three tragedians were selected to produce four plays apiece—three tragedies and one tragico-comedy known as a Satyric Drama. At the end of the performance a vote of the judges awarded the prize to one of the three competitors. Now, as a result of all this, Tragedy was still regarded as in some sort an act of worship. The characters appropriate for presentation were therefore heroes, demigods, or at least legendary figures; never contemporary personalities. This tendency to hark back upon the past is typical of the artistic restraint of the Greeks. Thus, when a temple was erected in honour of the Athenians' victories over the Spartans, the figured frieze around the cornice was made to represent not warriors of the day, but Persians fighting Greeks as in the great wars of fifty years before.* Then, again, the heroic figures around which the plays were written must for the purposes of tragedy be made to suffer; and the cause of their suffering was normally twofold. It is not to be found in their own innate flaws of character such as Othello's jealousy or Hamlet's irresolution; nor yet in the workings of a blind fate or an inscrutable Providence such as brought ruin upon King Lear. But it arose, in the first place, from a family curse such as the curse which ancestral crimes had imposed upon the House of Atreus in the *Agamemnon* or on the House of Oedipus in the *Antigone.* Secondly, this source of tragedy might be further supplemented or enhanced by an act of pride or presumption on the part of those who were to suffer. The Greeks were intensely superstitious in their dread of Nemesis, God's jealousy directed against the over-prosperous, more especially when they bore their good fortune in too self-

* This at least is the most probable account of the Temple of Victory on the Acropolis. The reader may note again how at the crisis of their two tragedies both Sophocles and Euripides after him make the Chorus escape, as it were, from the stress of their emotion by recalling to mind myths which bore a resemblance to the fates of Antigone and Medea.

confident a manner. Thus, Agamemnon's path to ruin is
specially prepared by the pride he displayed over the sack of
Troy and by his ultimate acceptance of the triumphal entry
which Clytamnestra offered him when he eached home.
Creon in the same way condemns himself, as it were, to a fall,
by the cavalier and haughty manner in which he sentences
Antigone to death. The theme of these two tragedies therefore
depends, like many others, on the dual working of Nemesis
and the ancestral curse.

In the plot equally there had grown up from the first a strong
tradition of common usage, due in no small measure perhaps
to the physical conditions of stage management under which
the dramas were actually produced. First and foremost the
Unities of Place and Time were very carefully observed ; that
is to say, the scene or place in which the plot was laid remained
the same throughout the whole play—there was no scene-
shifting ; and the time of duration was accepted as falling
within the compass of at most a single day. There were
exceptions to this rule. In the third and last play of the
Great Trilogy, of which the *Agamemnon* is the prelude, the
scene is shifted in the middle from Delphi to Athens. In the
Agamemnon itself, too, there are considerable difficulties about
the Unity of Time (see *Agamemnon*, Note 8). But none the
less the two rules normally held good. The development of
the plot further followed certain more or less definite conventional lines. Aeschylus, most of whose trilogies formed one
continuous whole with a single plot running throughout,
cannot here be taken as the norm ; but Sophocles, who preferred
to treat each of his three tragedies as a separate artistic unit,
established a sort of recognized canon or rule. The plot for
a while goes forward on uninterrupted and anticipated lines,
until about the middle occurs a sudden speeding-up, a hitch,
or unexpected reversal of circumstance. Creon is warned of
his impending fate by Teiresias and alters his mind about

Antigone. Medea is assured of safe sanctuary by King Aegeus and at once adopts a new scheme of revenge. The catastrophe follows sharp. The report of it is usually put into the mouth of a messenger ; for it was a further convention of Greek drama that no violent death should take place upon the stage. Then succeeds not infrequently a Death Tableau. The walls of the palace or temple, which formed the back-scene, roll back and disclose the murdered victim to the gaze of the actors and spectators. Violence, if shown at all, must be seen in repose, in its results, and not in the agitated movement of its occurrence. The highest pitch of emotion has now been touched ; and towards the close the Greek author preferred to strike a quieter key, the action dying away in a sort of serenity of philosophic sorrow. This again is typical of the artistic self-restraint of the Greeks. It does not readily commend itself to the more jaded tastes of modern times ; and even Shakespeare felt it necessary to satisfy his audience in their thirst for excitement by piling up the corpses at the close of *Hamlet* or giving them a battle at the ending of *Macbeth*.*

Such then were the main elements of Greek dramatic convention. But Euripides, though accepting them in many points, was no slave to them ; and he made one or two important new departures. In the first place he chose his subject-myth, as we have said, largely with an eye to its dramatic possibilities. Hence he was not readily content with the more hackneyed and familiar themes—though, like Aeschylus and Sophocles before him, he, too, produced a play about Electra—and he often went farther afield to the less well-known legendary tales. But here he was met by a difficulty. His audience might not be so well up as they should have been in the details of the story. Euripides, therefore, introduces a Prologue,† set as

---

* Feeling the inappropriateness of the quiet ending to modern production I have considerably curtailed the latter part of all three plays.

† The prologues preceding the *Agamemnon* and the *Antigone* are not of course drawn from the original text.

a rule in the mouth of some minor character such as the Nurse in the *Medea*; and by this method he was able to explain to the otherwise puzzled audience precisely how the situation lay. Then again Euripides made free use of another and less justifiable device. His plots have an awkward trick of becoming entangled at the close in some situation which appears impossible of solution. The fact is that he has up till this point pursued the course of the tragedy with persistent realism, intent on seeing for himself precisely how the situation would have worked out in actual everyday life, and caring very little where the method leads him. But, the method having led him into a dramatic *impasse*, he extricates himself by a swift return to the tradition of the legendary story. He introduces a god or goddess who settles matters, so to speak, by a wave of his or her wand, and so the play is satisfactorily ended. The *Deus ex machina* the device was called; because the deity was usually made to descend on a sort of primitive elevator or movable stage from the level of the palace roof.* There is no denying that Euripides overdid the use of it. For, truth to tell, he was not primarily interested in the construction of plots, so much as in the development of characters. There he easily outdistanced both his rivals; for they scarcely so much as attempted it. There is no change in Antigone's moods, no real emotional conflict; for she acts from a single impulse throughout. Clytamnestra, as we have said, is an incarnation of vindictiveness rather than a woman; we cannot picture her as feeling remorse, much less as showing it in her sleep like Lady Macbeth. But not so Medea; she is human, with human weaknesses and human moods. Clytamnestra resembles a mask set in one uniform, unalterable expression; but in the features of Euripides' characters are depicted all the changes of emotion, hope, anger, or despair, which serve to make them so wonderfully

* Medea is 'extricated' in a somewhat similar manner by giving her a fairy chariot to fly away in.

and pathetically alive. It is not difficult to understand why the people of the fourth century B.C. preferred Euripides to Aeschylus and Sophocles or to see why eighteen of his plays have been preserved against seven apiece of the other two. ' If I were sure that the dead survive,' said one of his ancient admirers, ' I would hang myself to see Euripides.'

III. THE CHORUS.

We have left the Chorus until last ; and yet in a sense we ought to have begun with it. For in the Chorus lay the whole origin of Greek Drama. In far-away years, before even Aeschylus was born or thought of, there had been held simple rustic festivals at which simple country dances had been danced and simple country songs sung in honour of Dionysus, god of the vintage, and the spirit of life-giving joy. In these ritual dances it had been the fashion, as with the psalm-singing Hebrews of old, to divide the chorus-band into two halves, which, as they danced, kept up a sort of antiphonal dialogue, each answering the other's song by turns. Such dialogue is a characteristic of primitive musical performances in many lands ; it is to be found in the old English folk-games which are still played by country children to this day ; yet in such dialogue lay the germ of Greek tragedy. For presently it came to pass that some individual—the author maybe of a newly invented song which was to be sung—stepped in and took a third part along with the two half-choruses, enacting in costume the rôle of a king or a demi-god, a prophet or a priest, perhaps even changing his costume and appearing in several characters by turn. This individual, in his fancy dress and make-believe impersonations, was the Actor in embryo. By and by, as time went on, a second actor was introduced ; then a third. There, however, the development stopped short. Even in the hey-day of Attic tragedy a play might never involve the introduction of more

than three characters simultaneously upon the stage. Many
parts indeed there might be; but only three actors to play
them, the change of disguise being effected behind the scene.
However that might be, the actors were by Aeschylus' time
a well-established element in drama; yet the chorus was still
at least equally important. In one of his plays as many as two-
thirds of the lines are assigned to them; and even in the
Agamemnon they occupy well over a third. In short, the drama
was still virtually a dancing performance with a mythical story
as its theme. Gradually, however, the balance was shifted;
and the chorus became subservient to the main plot as enacted
by the three individual players. It still sang and danced at
intervals, dividing itself, as in early days, into two bands,
which numbered six or seven members each, and there was
further a 'chorus-leader', who, when necessary, conversed
with the actors proper, and served as a spokesman for the whole
chorus. Now in some ways it is obvious that the continual
presence of a dozen or more persons throughout the play,
overhearing all the guilty secrets of dark conspirators, yet
forbidden by the necessities of the plot to divulge those secrets
to their intended victims, was at once incongruous, unreal,
and extremely embarrassing for the playwright. Nevertheless,
the convention was accepted both by author and audience;
and, having made this allowance, we can see that the chorus
was also capable of fulfilling a very useful function. It served
to punctuate the stages of the action (as the drop-curtain now
serves to divide scene from scene), but without the disadvantage
of arresting it entirely. It gave a convenient interval, during
which important events might be supposed to happen off the
stage (as, for instance, when the deaths of Antigone and Haemon
occur during the choric song in praise of Dionysus); and, above
all, it gave the poet an opportunity of commenting and moraliz-
ing upon the progress of the events in the play proper. The
relevance of these intermittent moralizations varies con-

siderably. In the *Antigone* the chorus digress to such general topics as the workings of Love or the history of the Rise of Man. In the *Medea*, they stick rather more closely to the matter immediately in hand. At any rate the poet himself did not consider he chorus an irrelevant or superfluous portion of the drama; for he must have expended a deal of trouble on the writing of these lyrical odes. Not merely are they often extremely beautiful, but their metrical arrangement is always extraordinarily complex and elaborate. Still, as in early days, the chorus danced and sang in two halves; and it was a tradition that the metrical system used by one half-chorus should be followed and reproduced to the minutest detail in the answer of the other half-chorus. The reader will gain some idea of the method from studying the lyrical dialogues which in the *Antigone* precede the heroine's final exit and Creon's farewell speech. There, but not elsewhere, I have advisedly attempted to imitate the exact balance of metrical system * which was an almost invariable characteristic of the choric songs of original Greek plays. In all the three dramatists, but in Euripides especially, apart from these choric songs proper, there is usually a large portion of the dialogue which is also lyrical in form; such lyrics occur as a rule at the more emotional crises of the play; and the actors must have chanted and even danced them as 'solos'. The fact is that the actors were beginning to usurp even the few functions left to the chorus; and bit by bit the chorus itself fell into disuse. In Aristophanes' last plays it has already almost disappeared. In later times it dropped out altogether; and in the Roman theatres the 'orchestra' or dancing-ring in which the chorus had performed its evolutions was given over to seats for the spectators. The name has survived, and is now applied to those unfortunate persons who still punctuate the intervals between the acts,

---

* And, incidentally, of rhyme, which of course does not appear in the Greek.

like the chorus of classical Greece, but to whose ineffectual melodies nobody any longer pays very much attention.

IV. ANCIENT PRODUCTION.

Greek plays were performed in an open-air theatre, the spectators sitting in a huge semicircular auditorium, carved, as a rule, out of the hillside. On the ground-level at the base of the auditorium was the circular dancing-ring or 'orchestra' in which the chorus performed its evolutions. Behind this and facing the auditorium rose the 'stage-buildings' or 'skênê', on which was painted or hung the representation of a palace or temple façade. In front of this the actors proper played their part, whether on a raised stage or on ground-level it is here unnecessary to inquire. There was at least one great central doorway leading into the supposed palace, often two side-doors flanking it, as well as entrances from the projecting wings of the building and entrances to right and left of the orchestra itself.*

The actors were dressed in a highly conventional costume. They wore face-masks, of a settled immovable expression, suited in some way to the character they played. These masks may possibly have assisted them, after the manner of a megaphone, in the difficult task of conveying the sound to the vast circle of spectators. Further, to increase their stature as befitted the heroic rôle they played, they wore high frontlets of hair, club-soled buskins, padded garments, and large gloves. The tragic actor in full war-paint was so astonishing and so alarming a spectacle that in inartistic Sparta, where a play was seldom witnessed, several women were said to have fainted outright at the first sight of them.

From all this it will at once be realized that Greek histrionic art was, like the other elements of the drama, highly conventional and restrained. Under such masks facial expression was

* It was an understood convention at Athens that characters entering from the immediate locality of the scene shown came in on the left, while those arriving from foreign parts came in on the right of the spectators.

impossible. In high-heeled buskins rapid movement would have been not merely indecorous, but positively dangerous. The actors, therefore, relied for producing their effects on excellence of elocution and ge ture. The lines were probably spoken in a high-pitched and well-sustained intonation, almost approximating to a chant. The gesture was probably confined to a series of more or less statuesque poses, equally sustained through considerable spaces of the recitative. The lyrical portions of the play were definitely sung—to the accompaniment of flute or lyre; and the dances which went with them were also of a conventional and traditional character, appropriate nevertheless to the subject-matter in hand, and perhaps even imitative of the idea expressed in the theme. Thus, a dirge might perhaps be accompanied by some such mimicry of a funeral *cortège* as may be seen in the folk-games above mentioned. It cannot, however, be pretended that we have much definite knowledge about the actual methods of the Greek dramatic artist. Nevertheless, it goes without saying that in order to reproduce at all adequately the masterpieces of ancient tragedy, we must study to preserve in some measure the unusual restraint and decorum, which were so manifestly the chief characteristic of their literary excellence. In Greece there were no Sarah Bernhardts or Sir Herbert Beerbohm Trees to give realistic imitations of sordid death agonies to the accompaniment of green limelight.

V. Modern Production.

From what has been said above, we may assert first of all that the method of acting Greek plays should differ considerably from that prevalent upon the modern stage. It should be far more restrained ; probably the lines should be spoken slowly, but with continuous rhythm, the sentence being taken rather as a whole than as a series of disconnected lines. Elocution and gesture should be closely studied; and gesture in particular should be free from the pernicious habit of constant and restless variety. There should be an appropriate pose for each sentence or passage;

but it should be maintained throughout the whole of that sentence or passage, somewhat after the manner of Oberon and Titania in Mr. Granville Barker's *Midsummer Night's Dream*. Better than superfluity of movement would be complete immobility. The Greeks were great admirers of the statuesque, and quiet acting, like studied silences, can be more effective than excessive agitation.

Clothing can be studied from any good reproduction of Greek vase-paintings, but the main characters of the play should be more elaborately and ornamentally dressed than the members of the chorus.

The chorus itself presents an obvious difficulty. Their grouping must be carefully thought out; else they will interrupt the view of the spectators. For this reason I have reduced their number in each play to four; but that is only a minimum In order to distribute the parts more evenly I have allowed each of the four a fair proportion of the choric odes; but this again can be varied at will.

The number of the actors, other than the chorus, can in like manner be arranged according to requirement. Three speaking actors (with a few ' supers ') can by the Greek method enact the entire play, changing their disguise rapidly behind the scenes.

The scenery presents little difficulty. A simple arrangement of curtains would suffice. I have, however, drawn a sketch of a Greek palace-front which might be manufactured with little difficulty. Detail of colour and decoration could be imitated from any illustrations of Greek architectural ornament. But proportion is more important than such detail.

The method of performing the choric odes is a serious problem. Should dancing be attempted, I feel pretty sure that actual figures of existing folk-dances should be adapted. It is impossible to invent anything equally effective. If such lines as the refrain in the *Agamemnon* should be actually sung, as I think they should, the music ought to be of a stately but mournful character. The Greeks themselves used somewhat primitive music, once again very conventional, since there were set 'modes' or scales appropriate to different choric themes. Probably Gregorian chants approach most nearly to the general character of their singing.

In conclusion, let me say that I am convinced that Greek plays are as well worth acting as those of Shakespeare or any other writer, and that their effect on a modern audience might be just as powerful. For there is, in reality, nothing 'dead' about the Classics; and it is precisely because their appeal is so universal that the plays still survive. Much has been done to prove this already at Bradfield and elsewhere. But to discover the most effective method of staging, elocution, and acting, requires a great deal more thought and imagination than has yet been given. Each set of producers must start afresh and think out for themselves in what manner the spirit of original masterpieces of Aeschylus, Sophocles, and Euripides can be most successfully brought out.

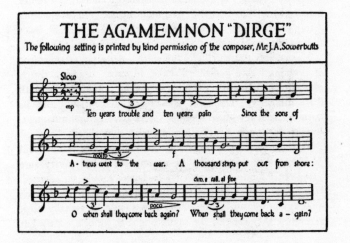

THE AGAMEMNON "DIRGE"

The following setting is printed by kind permission of the composer, Mr. J. A. Sowerbutts

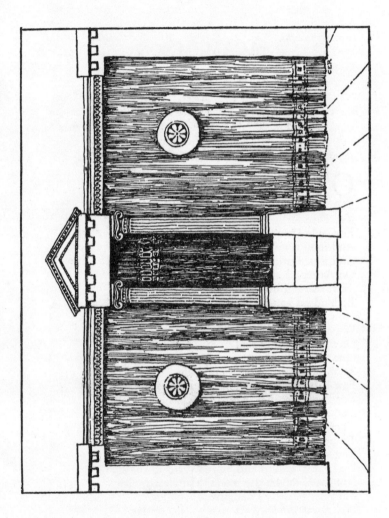

AGAMEMNON

DRAMATIS PERSONAE

AGAMEMNON, King of Argos.
CLYTAMNESTRA, his wife.
CASSANDRA, princess of Troy and
prisoner of Agamemnon.

A Sentinel.
A Messenger.
Chorus of Argive Elders.
Attendants, &c.

PROLOGUE

OF olden time, as you must understand,
The great prince, ATREUS, ruled in Hellas' land :
Mighty in peace was he and eke in war :
Yet Fate for him no pleasure had in store.
For he in God's despite did grievous sin,
And foulest murder wrought on his own kin.
And, since from one ill deed is gotten worse,
On ATREUS' lineage was laid this curse :
That doom'd his seed should be perpetually
By kindred hand a violent death to die.   10
Now of this ATREUS were two princes sprung,
Whose fame was loud on every Grecian tongue ;
One, MENELAUS, ruled in Sparta broad,
One, AGAMEMNON, was of Argos lord.
Anon it fell that MENELAUS' wife
Fair lady HELEN brought upon Greece great strife ;
For PARIS won her heart to lawless joy,
And she with him fled faithless off to Troy.
Then did the brothers twain in wrath conspire
To punish PARIS and burn Troy with fire.   20
Yet, as the warriors muster'd dight for war,
Up sprang a wind and bound them to the shore ;
Nor could aught else to stay the blast suffice
But AGAMEMNON's daughter's sacrifice.
Loath was the king his lovely child to slay :
But strong was Fate, nor dared he but obey.

That deed of shame what boots it to rehearse ?
From one ill done is gotten other worse :
On ATREUS' lineage fell again the curse.

For that day's sacrifice brought anguish keen   30
On CLYTAMNESTRA, AGAMEMNON's queen :
And blood with blood then plann'd she to reward
And visit vengeance on her guilty lord.
Ten years he tarried in Troy's distant clime ;
Ten years they fought ('tis writ in Homer's rime) :
And ten long years the queen abode her time.

So when the fullness of the days was come,
And AGAMEMNON sail'd victorious home,
No true love's welcome did await him there
But dark conspiracy and treacherous snare.   40
For with AEGISTHUS' aid, her secret lover,
The queen wove wiles her dark intent to cover.
Her husband lured she in with fondest show,
Flung garments over him, then to and fro
Swung her bright axe, and fell'd him at a blow.

So AGAMEMNON died, as Heaven will'd ;
The curse of ATREUS was again fulfill'd.
Yet for that guilty house no rest might be,
And blood for blood was still the gods' decree.
Her daughter's death in full the queen requited ;   50
But thence the doom on her own head alighted.
Nor could aught else for that dark deed atone,
Save kindred hand repeat what kindred hand had done,
And murd'ress murder'd be by him that was her son.

*The scene is laid before Agamemnon's palace in Argos.
    A flight of steps leads up to the central doorway, which
    is hung with a heavy curtain. Beside the steps stands
    a sentinel. It is the twilight before dawn.*

SENTINEL (*raising his head wearily*). God !
I'm aweary of this watch.   Year in, year out

I've done my sentry-go at the palace gate,
Couch'd chin on elbow like a kennelled dog,
Till I know the stars o' th' midnight sky by rote,
All the merry masters of the firmament,
That bring us frost and summer in their seasons,
Winking aloft in space.—For here I'm set
To mark the fire signal that brings the news
Of Troy town's capture ;—slave to a woman's whim
That hopes 'gainst hope and takes no gainsaying.   10
So for me 'tis watch, watch, watch, early and late
Drench'd by the dews, and never a sweet dream
To break my vigil.   For the dread of her
Stands ever at my elbow banning sleep,
Lest sleep should close mine eyes for evermore.
Times are when ever and anon I'll fall
To whistling or a-humming some old song ;
Sleep's antidote, the charm for the drowsy lids ;
But the tune turns quick to sorrow, and tears rise
For the thought of my master's house so sorely stricken, 20
And its ancient glory vanished.   Heaven send
A happy issue from our present trouble,
When the fire's message shall shine out of the dark,
And the glad news be sped.
[*He relapses into silence.   Presently from the wings a light
    flickers, then burns to a steady blaze.*]
                              Hail, blessed beacon !
Herald of the dawn that shall set Argos dancing
For this day's happiness. [*Turning to the palace.*] Ho
    there within !
I must get me straight to Agamemnon's mistress
And bear her tidings that she rise in haste
To rouse the echoes with her song of jubilee,
If Troy indeed be ta'en, and the beacon's true.   30
Marry ! I could shift myself to tread a measure ;
So fairly hath Dame Fortune cast the dice
For my old master. 'Faith, 'tis a treble six.[1]
But give me his hand to clasp when he comes home,

His hand in my hand for the love I bear him.
O' th' rest—I'm dumb ; my tongue is weighed, as though
An ox bestrid it. Yet had these walls speech,
What tales they might be telling. He who knows
May take my meaning ; who knows not—no more ;
My thought is gone whence it had come before.   40
                              [*He enters the palace door.*]

*After a slight pause, enter a Chorus of four Elders from the
wing. As they come they chant a mournful refrain.*

   ALL (*singing*).
Ten years' trouble, and ten years' pain,
Since the sons of Atreus went to the war.
A thousand ships put out from shore ;
O when shall they put back again ?

   1ST ELDER (*speaking*).
For Atreus' sons the Lord on high
Ordained a far and perilous quest,
All for the sake of a graceless guest
And a wife's disloyalty ;

That Greece should taste war's bitterness,
   Troy hear the battle's thunder ;   50
Where man grips man in the heat of the press
And knees are bowed for weariness
   And the spear is knapp'd in sunder.

   2ND ELDER.
Yet the princes' voyage God prospered not,
   (Ah me) for all their hasting.
For out of the east came a wind, I wot,
And storm-bound they lay till their ships did rot,
   And the flower of Greece was wasting.

Then spake the seer a bitter word,
   How the sea might yet be passed ;   60
And at that the chiefs were sad for their lord,
And with their staves they smote on the sward
   And ever the tears flowed fast.

3RD ELDER.

Then spake the king, ' O Fate is cruel,
   Since, ere we pass the water,
A father's hand must pile the fuel
And a father's hand must take the tool
   To sacrifice his daughter.'

Her father in vain the maid besought,
   In vain she pleaded sore,   70
But in his soul fell madness wrought,
And the price of her young life was naught
   To those grim lords of war.

4TH ELDER.

Her lips they bound with a silken thong
   And her arms with a hangman's halter.
O the maid was weak and the murderers strong,
But her look could speak, though hush'd her tongue,
And it pierced their hearts with the shame of their wrong
   As they laid her down on the altar.

What followed then, I dare not tell.   80
Dark 's the deed, and dark the spell.
   For those that did that murder foul
Must bear for aye the curse of hell ;
   And God have mercy on their soul.

ALL (*singing*).
      Ten years' trouble, and ten years' pain,
      Since King Agamemnon went to the war.
      His way was won, but the cost was sore.
      What way shall he come back again ?

As day begins to dawn, CLYTAMNESTRA *appears at the
palace door, and seeing the Elders halts upon the head
of the steps. The* FIRST ELDER, *with an obeisance,
accosts her.*

1ST ELDER. At thy summons, Clytamnestra, we are
come; A queen's word is sovereign, when her lord's away.

Yet were we fain to learn what news is this 91
That calls for sacrifice—good news or ill ?
> CLYTAMNESTRA. Night is kind, but her daughter Dawn
> is kinder.[2]
Good news that far outstrips thy fondest hope.
Priam's city is in Argive hands.
> 1ST ELDER. What hast thou said ? or do my ears prove
> liars ?
> CLY. Great Troy is ours—a plain tale plainly told.
> 1ST ELDER. What token hast thou that the thing is
> certain ?
> CLY. Sure token have I ; else is God a cheat.
> 1ST ELDER. The sea is wide ; what messenger so swift
That he might cross it ? 101
> CLY. On Ida's slope the Fire-God lit the flame.[3]
Beacon sped beacon hitherward from Troy,
And the fire ran courier. Ida passed it on
To the wild cliffs of Lemnos. Far away
God's mount, tall Athos, caught the island gleam
And, towering heaven-high to span the ocean,
Her beacon, like a sun in golden glory,
Signalled the message to Makistos' summit.
He tarried not nor slumbered, but performed 110
His herald's duty. By Euripus' stream
The sentinels were ware of it ; and straight
Shone forth their answering conflagration
Kindled of withered bracken set in store.
On, on ; the flame unwearying, undimmed
O'erleapt Asopus' meads. Beyond Gergopis
The bright beam soared, bidding them serve the fire
On Aegiplanctus. A great beard of flame
Was wafted thence to overtop the headland
Where the cliffs look down on the Saronic waters ; 120
Till last it lighted on yon neighbouring peak,
Our Arachnaeus ; and the palace-hall
Of Atreus' sons shone with the signal-fire
That looks to Ida for its ancestry.

There have you all; that is my proof and token
Sent by my lord from the plains of captured Troy.
   Cho. Praise be to God! Thine, lady, is a tale
That I could hear twice told, yet joy to hear it.
   Cly. This night the Argives bivouac in Troy.
Methinks I hear the shouting—strange confusion—   130
Two elements mingling, yet no more commingled
Than oil can mix with vinegar. The children,
Seeing a father or a brother dead,
Raise lamentation, while they hug the corpse
And know themselves for slaves. Hard by the victors,
Worn with the night's work and ravenous
From the long fast of hungry battle stand not
On ceremony, but set them down pell-mell [4]
To taste the city's viands. Trojan roofs
Perforce must yield them shelter. They forget   140
The dews under the starlight and the ache
Of numbing frosts; and sleep like happy warriors
Unbroken slumber all the livelong night.
O, if in their triumph's hour they stay the hand,
And touch nor shrine nor altar of the Gods [5]
They've conquered, then the residue is safe,
Fate cannot touch them.
   1st Elder.   Lady, 'tis well said;
And, since thy proofs are such that none may question,
I'll offer thanks for this great victory.

The Chorus raise hands skywards; and, as they offer their
    prayer, a travel-stained messenger bearing the herald's
    staff enters from the left.

   Messenger. O Argos, home of my fathers, I am come,
A ten years' truant; many hopes have foundered   151
But this sole prayer is granted. Little thought I
To lay my bones in Argos when I died.
But now all hail! Hail, my belovéd country!
Hail, Sun! Hail, Zeus! Hail, Phoebus!—Ah cruel
   damage

Thou wroughtest us beside Scamander's stream.[6]
(*Turning to* CHORUS.) Hark ye, good sirs ! Know ye that
  Agamemnon
Comes home to-day, bringing sunshine in his train
To one and all in Argos ?
  1ST ELDER.   Herald of the host,
God's blessing on thee.
    MESS.   For that word much thanks. 160
Now even death itself hath lost its bitterness.
  1ST ELDER. Amen to that. What 's death at such an
    hour ?
  MESS. Let be ! All 's well. Yet could I but recount
Half what we've suffered—the bivouac by night
Under the foeman's wall ; the heavy moisture
That rotted the foul garments on our back ;
Nights that no bird could live through ; aye and then
The scorching heat when the sea sat motionless
Lapped in the bosom of the sleeping noon,
And no breath stirred. But that 's all past ; why wake 170
Forgotten memories ? Even the dead forget
Their lust to live again.—Old friends, farewell !
And for us living this day's happiness
Shall know no flaw. 'Tis yours to bless the city
And to greet our captain at his homecoming.
  1ST ELDER. Thy words undo me quite ; yet that great
    prince
To honour fitly is Clytamnestra's care.
  CLYTAMNESTRA (*descending from the palace steps*).
A song of praise I sang from my heart's flow
When first the midnight signal was announced,
Telling our victory and the sack of Troy ;   180
Now must I go to set in readiness
The welcome for my lord. (*She moves up the steps again,*
  then turns). Yet tell him this—
Argos hath smiles for him. (*She again mounts the steps,*
  but again turns). And tell him too
How loyal a wife he shall find waiting here,

As when he left her, watchful as a dog
To spy out enemies and guard the home,
Keeping her troth unspotted through the years.
Never a breath of scandal have I known ;
Never to men's flattery have been familiar.
For suchlike artifice I have no skill   190
            (*She pauses and the messenger goes out.*)
No more than for the tempering of steel.[7]   [*Exit.*]

    The CHORUS *take up their refrain again :*
God is jealous ; but God is just,
And his vengeance falls where guilt hath been.
For man must pay the price of sin
Till his pride be humbled in the dust.

    1ST ELDER (*speaking*).
Menelaus, Sparta's lord,
In Lacedaemon held his sway ;
There Paris came with heart of fraud,
Nor kept the law of friendship's board,
    But stole his lovely wife away.   200
She left the hall, she left the bower,
    To pass the threshold over.
O, beauty's sweets were turned to sour,
When she brought on Greece war's evil hour,
And tears to Troy for a wedding-dower,
    And a sword to slay her lover.

    2ND ELDER.
Ah me ! Ah me, for a home forlorn !
    Ah me, for a husband's sorrow !
For him a desolate couch to mourn,
And the empty corridor's silent scorn,   210
    And the dawn of a hopeless morrow.
In dreams he would follow the phantom bright
    Of her that had travelled the deep ;
But or ever he won to his soul's delight,
It had vanished and gone from the paths of sight
    On the gossamer wings of sleep.

3RD ELDER.

O women must weep, when the watch-fires burn,
For their life's joy gone on the gust,
For their living lord shall never return,
But in his stead a burial urn,   220
And a handful of mouldering dust.

For the God of War is a merchant deft;
And his hands hold weighted scales.

In costly wares he trafficketh
And the bargain he drives is a bargain with Death
And the bodies of men are his bales.

4TH ELDER.

O bitter, bitter the battle's fruit!
And its seed is sown in the grave.

Now many a voice is hushed and mute
In a far land over the wave.   230

So endeth Troy's prosperity.
Her towers lie level with the sod.

For whoso setteth his horn on high
And behaveth himself frowardly
Shall learn, I ween, before he die,
The power of the wrath of God.

ALL (*singing*).

God is jealous; but God is just.
Envy waits on fortune's hour;
Vengeance follows reckless power;
And Pride is humbled in the dust.   240

A flourish of trumpets is heard without; and AGAMEMNON
enters with two attendants. Behind him follows
CASSANDRA, *the princess of Troy, whose fate it is to*
foretell the future with unerring instinct, but never be
believed. Her arms are manacled. The Elders make
obeisance.

AGAMEMNON. O Gods of Argos, Gods of this dear
country,[8]

Yours be the praise for my safe home-coming,
And for the debt by Priam duly paid.
Proud Troy smokes heavenwards; and over it
The winds of fate blow bare. Then praised be God
That for a woman's sake the sons of Argos
Have laid the town in ruin, breaching the wall
What time the Pleiads [9] set. (*Turning to the Elder who spoke last.*)

And as for thee
I accept thy homage; and what thou saidst I heard.
My thought 's as thine. Few among mortal men   250
Escape that canker of prosperity—
Envy. Myself have known and no man better
The fair-day friendship that to th' eye 's all smiles,
But harbours inwardly sour discontent
Against another's fortune. O, 'tis a mask,
The loyal heart's counterfeit, affection's ghost.
Give me not such to love me.—Now for matters
Of more present moment. We must here consult
With what burnt-offering or sacrifice
We may appease that jealous power on high   260
That frowns on man's success.

CLYTAMNESTRA (*who has entered as he speaks*). O Citizens,
I do not blush to tell you of the love
I bear my husband. All the weary while
He was away, I have eaten out my heart
In widowed loneliness. As years sped by,
Came rumours, ill tale-bearers of ill news,
That he was dead, was wounded. Had the wounds
Been half so numerous as by report
I had it, then were his poor body pierced
More full of holes, I trow, than is a net.[10]   270
Night was one long vigil. If I slept
The droning gnat would wake me with its flutter;
And in my fitful dreams I'd see thee run
Hazards far exceeding the brief time's compass.
But now thou art returned; and I would hail thee

Husband, friend, stout watch-dog of the fold,[11]
The ship's sheet-anchor, pillar of the house
That stays the beaméd roof, welcome as day
To ship-wrecked mariners when hope is lost
Or as water-spring to traveller in the waste.   280
And now, dear husband, enter to thy rest.
Open before thee lies the door. Yet stay!
Not on dull earth shall the foot that trod Troy under
Be planted here. [*She motions the attendants to spread
     a carpet which lies at the stair head.*] Up, up, ye
     laggards! Spread
The path before him with a tapestry
Of purple damask. Soft shall be the way,
That leads our lord and master to a homing
Such as he never dreamt of.
          AGAMEMNON.   Leda's daughter,[12]
What thou hast said in welcome, was well said.
I blame 't in no wise. But with purple trappings   290
And woman's trump'ry gauds what have I to do?
Am I some princeling of the Orient [13]
To tread on carpets and affect to prize
The empty courtesies of grovelling crowds?
Tempt me not. For that way lies the curse
Which waits on pride. God is a jealous god;
No man is safe till life be safely ended;
And such be my end!
          CLY.   Thou shalt not say me nay.
     AG. My purpose stands.
          CLY.   Thou fear'st man's censure then?
     AG. Even the murmurings of the crowd have weight.
     CLY. Even a conqueror for once may yield.   301
     AG. Hath such a paltry triumph so great charms?
     CLY. The boon is nothing. Humour me thus far.
     AG. Have then thy way this once, woman. Come, slave,
Loose me my sandals. (*Pointing to* CASSANDRA) As for yon
     stranger lass,
Handle her kindly. Her the army gave me,

Flower of the captives, choicest of the spoil,
To be my hand-maiden. What soul is fain
For bondage? Mercy doth become the victor.
God reward me, as I have used her well.   310
And, as I pass the threshold purple-strewn,
Envy avaunt! Peep not, ye spiteful fates.
    CLY. A sea there is (and who shall staunch its flow?)
Where wells a precious fount of blood-red ooze
Man's vesture to incarnadine.[14] O King,
Thy house is rich, thank God, in suchlike treasure;
I'ld not stint it. For thy life given back
Is more to me than many household stuffs.
[AGAMEMNON *enters*; CLYTAMNESTRA *lingers for an
    instant.*]
O hear me, mighty Zeus to whom men pray.
All power is thine; grant me my prayer this day.   320
[CLYTAMNESTRA *enters the palace-door, the curtains closing
    behind her.* CASSANDRA *is left standing as if in thought,
    and strangely silent.*]

    CHORUS (*singing*).
Now welcome pleasure, and farewell pain!
For the voyage is sped and the battle is won,
And the weary watching is over and done,
When the king comes home again.

    2ND ELDER.
O'er the Place of the Curse, where the ships lay moored,
The sands of the years drift deep.
Yet the years tarry long for a true prophet's word;
And there surgeth within me a terror untoward,
    Like a sign from the visions of sleep.

    3RD ELDER.
Glad cheer they have brought us from over the seas,
Glad cheer to all beholding.   331
But is it a death-knell is borne on the breeze,
Or the throb of a heart that is robbed of its ease
    By a dark foreboding?

4TH ELDER.
O wild are the waves the vessel must ride,
Where lurk the cruel rocks under;
Then beware of the perilous portion of pride,
And fling out the rich freight from the good ship's side
Or surely she shall founder.

ALL (*singing*).
Welcome to pleasure! Farewell to pain!   340
Yet my heart yearns sore for a maiden dead—
Life-blood spilt and spirit fled,
    O who shall call them back again ?

CLYTAMNESTRA (*reappearing*). Cassandra, get thee in.
    Stand not thus proudly.
In olden time even Alcmena's son
Bore, so they say, the yoke of bondage. Come ;
Such fare as custom sanctions thou shalt have.
    1ST ELDER. 'Tis to thee my mistress speaks. Lend her
        thine ear.
The toils of fate are round thee ; best submit.
    CLY. Unless her speech be some outlandish jargon 350
Like a swallow's twitter,[15] she cannot mistake me.
But I'll not dally here to brook her scorn.   [*Exit.*]
    1ST ELDER. Poor maid, I cannot find it in my soul
To speak thee harshly. Yet must thou bend the neck
And shoulder the burden of necessity.
    CASSANDRA. Oh ! Oh ! Oh !
O God ! God ! God !
    1ST ELDER. Why dost thou call God's name thus plain-
        tively ?
    CASS. O God ! God ! God !   359
Whither hast thou brought me ? What are these halls ?
    1ST ELDER. Yonder is the palace-hall of Atreus' line.
    CASS. Ah, no, accurséd spot ! It is a charnel-house
Crammed with foul secrets ; and on the floor is blood.
    1ST ELDER. Like a hound upon the scent, the weird
        enchantress

Snuffs murder in the wind.

CASS.   O horror! horror! horror!

That one so dear should so plot upon her dearest.

1ST ELDER. What, riddling yet; I have no skill to take
thee.

CASS. (*pointing in the air*). Aha! What instrument is
that ? A net!

A snare to catch and hold—in the hand of a friend.

And a death-dirge I hear of many voices   370

Moaning on the wind.

1ST ELDER. What hellish spectre haunts thy vision now ?

That speech mislikes me, and my blood runs chill

Drop by slow drop, as from a mortal wound

At the red life's ebbing.

CASS.   Look! Look! There the bull

Staggers. His mate has struck him. Under the blow

Of those cruel horns he falls and falls and falls.

1ST ELDER. With these strange visions I am quite be-
mused.

And follow her but darkly.

CASS.   O, the doom

Peeps not from curtains like a new-wed bride :   380

But clear as wind at dawn it surges up

Against the sunrise. I'll have done with riddles.

Over this house hover the fiends of hell ;

To give them heart withal they have drunk deep

Of human blood. There sit they high and chaunt

Their awful anthem ; and none evermore

Shall move them from these halls. O mine's a
tongue

Which cannot lie. To me God gave the gift

Of true prognostication.[16]

1ST ELDER.   Doubt I dare not,

There's more in this than idle babblers use.   390

CASS. O woe! Again the fit comes over me.

There stands the she-wolf, lolls a tongue and fawns

In cringing courtesy—and murder at her heart.

How shall I call thee ? Basilisk ? or Scylla [17]
Couch'd mid the rocks to prey on mariners ?
Nay, Hell's own dam whose baleful breath blasts friend
And foe alike. O list you well. Within
Those doors I travel to the utterance
Of mine own dirge and his, who was your king.

 1st Elder. Hush ! leave that word unspoken.
 Cass.   He shall die ;
And I die with him ; nor am I fain to live.   401
Death's portals ope before me. All I pray
Is that the end be easy. Troubles cease
When the blood letting's done, and eyes are closed in peace.

 1st Elder. Fortune comes, and Fortune goes ;
      But the hour of his passing no man knows.
 2nd Elder. Yet wealth disdains to curb its lust
      Till pride be humbled in the dust.
 3rd Elder. Priam's city hath he ta'en
      And princely cometh home again.   410
 4th Elder. But whoso sheddeth man's blood, 'tis said,
      By man in turn shall his blood be shed.

        [Cassandra *enters the Palace.*]

 Agamemnon (*within*). O ! O, a mortal blow—in the house of my friends.

 4th Elder. Hark ! what is that voice in agony of death ?

 Agam. And yet again. O, I am lost, lost, lost.

 1st Elder. What deed is this ? It is the king's voice. Quick.
What 's ours to do ?

 2nd Elder.   I' Faith, it were securer
To wake the city with a cry to arms.

 3rd Elder. That 's not my thought. We should be up and doing
To take the guilty in their bloody act.   420

 4th Elder. I too am with thee. 'Tis no time for parley.

2ND ELDER. Stay, stay ! Be cautious ; for the queen's
spies, doubt not,
Are ranging through the city.
3RD ELDER. Idle talk !
Words cannot bring the dead to life again.
4TH ELDER. Who cares to outlive this day, our master
gone ?
1ST ELDER. Whether he be living or already dead
We have no certitude.
ALL. In, in ; we'll know the truth.

As the Elders approach the door, the curtain is suddenly with-
drawn and reveals CLYTAMNESTRA *standing, axe in hand.*

CLYTAMNESTRA. No shame I think it to unsay the words
Wherewith aforetime I have lulled suspicion,
T' encompass my victim in the cunning snare.   430
Long I planned, sure was my triumph. First,
A web of silken cloth I flung about him,
Caught like a fish, and struggling in the meshes,
I struck him thus and thus. Two groans he gave,
Then bowed him at my feet ; there, as he lay,
I smote him yet a third time. Thrice they say
A man must call upon the Lord of Death [18]
Before he 's answered. So his spirit fled
And on those dying lips the bright blood jetting
Tinted my vesture with its crimson spume.   440
O welcome to me was that sprinkled shower
As to parched fields sweet rain in summer time.
Grieve, an ye will ; or, an ye will, be glad.
To me this deed brings joy unspeakable.
1ST ELDER. Woman, what poison hath bewitched thy
sense ?
Or of what potent drug from ocean's flow
Hast thou drunk deep,—to drench the world in blood
And make thyself abhorréd of mankind ?
CLY. Dost thou reproach me ? Such words touch me
not.

With him the burden lies who thought no shame   450
To slay his daughter, offspring of my womb,
As she had been some kid out of the fold,
To stay the winds of Thrace.
    1st Elder.   Wrath maddens thee.
Yet surely as thy stroke hath laid him low,
Thy life is forfeit. Blood aye calls for blood.
    Cly. My child's avenged. What care I for thy
      threats ?
My own Aegisthus, the comrade of my heart,[19]
Shall keep my home secure. (*She draws aside the curtain,*
    and discloses the bodies of Agamemnon *and* Cassandra.)
                Come, look on him,
Look on the guilty partner of his couch,
His darling prophetess, his fondled toy,   460
And know my just revenge. There side by side
The lovers twine in death. No rarer spice
Can enhance the luxury of a woman's feast
Than her supplanter's ruin.
    1st Elder.   It is the Curse,
The Curse that overhangs continually
The House of Atreus, and like a carrion bird
Gluts its foul appetite on dead men's blood.
    Cly. Aye ; call not this deed mine. Thou seest here
No wife of Agamemnon, mortal clay,[20]
But an avenging spirit sent from heaven,   470
To wreak God's vengeance on a guilty line.
There works the Curse, not I. My hands are clean.
    1st Elder. Murderess yet thou art, though fiends of hell
Have nerved thy sinews, and through thee have wrought
To bring my lord and master to the grave.
Would God the earth had oped and swallowed me
Before mine eyes beheld him lying so—
Who shall lament him ? Who his tomb prepare,
And say over his ashes the last requiem ?
    Cly. By my hand he fell—and by my hand   480
He shall be buried. Beside the Ghostly River

His daughter, Iphigeneia, shall fling wide
Her arms, and give him greeting with the kiss
Of death. It is enough, my friends; for so
Is the long doom ended, and the House quit
Of that dread Curse which hath encompassed it.

[The curtains close again.]

1ST ELDER.
Orestes lives! Son dares, as dareth mother; [21]
And one foul deed of blood begets another.

ALL.
Orestes lives.

2ND ELDER.
They have taken the whelp of a lioness; 490
Wean'd it and bred it at home,
The toy of the children's kindness
The joy of the old men's blindness,
    Till the fullness of time be come.

Those mild eyes who could have dreaded,
    Those soft mild eyes which fawn
On the hand of the friend that has fed it,
While it lies in the arms that have bred it
    As gentle as babe new-born?

But the son of the old lion's daughter 500
    His debt shall at last make good.
Will he stay for his master's order—
To be filling the house with slaughter
    And the home with a welter of blood?

ALL (*singing*).
Pain and trouble; trouble and pain.
    Slow is the spirit of man to learn.
But the hand of God is hard to turn;
And, as a man soweth, he reaps again. [22]

[Exeunt singing.]

ANTIGONE

DRAMATIS PERSONAE

CREON, King of Thebes.
EURIDICE, his wife.
ANTIGONE and ISMENE, his nieces.
HAEMON, his son and lover of
    Antigone.

TEIRESIAS, a blind prophet.
A Guard.
Attendants, Guide of Teiresias,
    &c.
Chorus of Theban Elders.

PROLOGUE

ON many an ancient did the hand of Fate
  Bring grievous sorrow, smiting soon or late;
But none more sad than OEDIPUS, I ween,
The unhappy son of Theban king and queen.
For, born in sorrow, and as babe outcast,
His fate it was, when home he came at last,
Not knowing who he was nor what he did,
To slay his father and his mother wed.
Set on Thebes' throne great glory then was his;
None dreamt what horror underlay his bliss.   10
Time sped; well on in years, he learnt the truth,
The secret sin of his unwitting youth.
Then the wife-mother, innocent-guilty dame,
Slew her own self to cancel her own shame;
And, fool of Fate, by Fate made tardy wise,
The King, fordone with grief, thrust out his eyes.
An exile blind, by his two daughters led,
ISMENE and ANTIGONE, he fled;
Till Death bestowed the rest for which he yearned,
And home to Thebes the sisters twain returned.   20
Yet on that home the Curse was now renewed,
And their two brothers were at open feud.
So hot the strife, that POLYNEICES fled,
Yet vowed swift vengeance on his brother's head.
In far lands mustered he a mighty host.
Many lent aid; the king of Argos most.

So Seven Princes came in rich array
Sworn to take Thebes and ETEOCLES to slay.
Rash was their boast, and vain the reckless vow ;
The men of Thebes rolled back that haughty foe.　　30
Yet so it fell, ere that sad day was over,
That POLYNEICES in combat met his brother.
Amain they fought, the one to save his town,
The one with treason foul to cast her down.
Each found his mark, thrust home the guilty brand,
And each lay murdered by a brother's hand.
So died they : and proud CREON was monarch in the land.

*The scene is laid before the royal palace at Thebes. Enter
the two daughters of* OEDIPUS, ISMENE *and* ANTIGONE.

　　ANTIGONE. 'Tis a weary life, Ismene, sister mine ;
And the woes of Oedipus are multiplied
On us his children. We have drunk the cup
Of shame and sorrow and calamity
Even to the dregs ; and now through the common ways
Runs whisper of a savage ordinance
Foreboding wicked work to our beloved.
Hast heard so ?
　　ISMENE.　　Be it good or be it ill,
Rumour for me is hushed, Antigone,
Since on one same sad day in mortal fight　　10
Our two dear brothers died. The Argive host
Is this night gone, I know ; yet know no more
Whether for weal or woe.
　　ANT.　　　　Ah, so methought ;
And therefore have I fetched thee here to hold
A word in secret.
　　ISM.　　　　Sister, what is this
So stirs the tranquil waters of thy soul ?
　　ANT. Those brothers twain for whose sad loss we grieve,
Creon, our captain, hath variously consigned
To honour and dishonour. Eteocles
Shall have due portion with the honoured dead　　20

And decent rite of hallowed burial ; [1]
But Polyneices' piteous corse is laid
Under a ban of general proclamation,
That none shall say his dirge nor dig his grave,
But all unhousell'd and unwept he lie
To glut foul carrion birds with his sweet flesh.
And, whoso disregardeth the decree,
The folk shall stone that soul to bloody death.
Now make thy choice ; for here the chance doth lie
To shew thy mettle, or degeneracy.   30
   Ism. Alas, poor sister, since it must be so,
What strength have I to answer yes or no ?
   Ant. I need thy hand to aid me in the task.
   Ism. What work is toward ? Wherefor dost thou
    ask ?
   Ant. My work it is to sepulchre the dead.
   Ism. Our brother bury—and he a man forbid ?
   Ant. My brother then ; no need to call him thine ;
I'll be no traitor to my kith and kin.
   Ism. Defy the law ? O mad and desperate whim !
   Ant. No law can come betwixt myself and him.   40
   Ism. O sister, of the troublous past bethink thee,
Our father's sin by his own search reveal'd,
Our father's eyes by his own hand outscor'd,
Mother in self-abhorrence self-destroyed,
Brothers in mutual slaughter jointly slain,
And we two left alone in a lonely world,
How can we brave the tyrant's wrath and live,
Frail weakly women matched against hard males,
And nature's subjects against sovereign power ?
To outstep reason were defect of reason ;   50
There is no sense in it.
   Ant. I am not importunate. Be what thou wilt.
Mine is a happier lot, to bury him
And die. For better far to serve the dead
Than serve the living ; with the dead hereafter
We must abide to all eternity.

Ism. O, I am fearful how it shall befall.

Ant. Look to thyself, fear not for me at all.

Ism. Let us be secret. Breathe not thine intent.

Ant. Go, blazen it broadcast to the firmament ;   60
No voice I heed but one.

Ism.   It may not be ;
Thy hollow hope is set on vanity.

Ant. Till strength be done, I'll hope and then despair.

Ism. Best never woo a hope that leads thee—where ?
Yet go, if go thou must—who ever knew
A quest so witless, or a heart so true ?

Enter a chorus of four Theban Elders.

1st Elder.
Dawn, whose bright eye peeps forth by Dircê's marge,[2]
　Ne'er beamed more radiant through the saffron dome
Than when the warrior of the silvern targe [3]
　Turned in confusion home.   70

Like ravenous eagle with a rending cry,
　Before the city's battlement he stood,
Her bulwarks tall with flaming torch to ply
　And drench her stones in blood.

The pride of chivalry, the pomp of ringing gold
　Surged up defiant to the siegéd door ;
Then in the Dragon wrath kindled, and behold ! [4]
　The foe was found no more.

2nd Elder.
Came seven princes to our seven ports [5]
　Which seven trusty captains held in ward ;   80
Till fell for vengeance on their guilty thoughts
　The fury of the Lord.

But two there were of the same loins sprung,
　Two brethren suckled at one mother's breast ;
Each against each his gleaming falchion swung
　And clove a brother's crest.

Yet loud, ye Thebans, lift the triumph song !
  And tune your voices to a psalm of praise.
Lead forth the dancing ; for the night is long,
  And the God walks the ways.[6]   90

  3RD ELDER.
Lo, yonder comes the king, that we may gather
For what intent we have been summoned hither.

        Enter CREON.

God hath been merciful, ye men of Thebes,
To salve the storm-racked vessel of our State ;
And, since that Oedipus' two sons are fallen
The mutual victims of intestine feud,
I am by right of consanguinity [7]
Exalted to the throne. Know then my will
As touching them, how I have made decree
That Eteocles, the faithful friend of Thebes   100
And her proved champion in this sad affray,
Shall in a holy tomb lie consecrate,
As his late valiance fits ; but Polyneices,
That double traitor who from outlawry
Turned back to set her pinnacles ablaze
And batten on her blood, him I declare
Attainted and proclaimed that none be forward
To grant his body rites of sepulture,
But he be left a stark, unhallowed thing
For birds and dogs to peck at. Such am I,   110
Firm friend to loyal hearts—above, below ;
But to all traitors an unrelenting foe.
    1ST ELDER. 'Tis my lord's good pleasure. Let thy word
      be law,
There 's none in Thebes hath power to question it.
    CREON. See then ye give good heed to mark its breach.
    1ST ELDER. We are too old ; look out some younger
      man.
    CREON. The watch is ordered. The corse hath sentinels.

Yet, be one bold this edict to defy
Take not nor lot nor part with him ; or ye shall die.

Enter the Guard.

My liege, I would not claim   120
To have posted hither in a panting haste ;
For on my path I turned me oft about
To hold self-converse with my thought-packed soul.
' Fool ', quoth sage soul, ' why foot it forth so fast
Upon an errand that will work thee woe ? '
' On, madman ! ' counterwise said soul again,
' Let but the king learn this from other lips,
And thou'lt pay dear for it.' Communing thus
In cautious zeal and hot-paced sluggardry
My road's brief-tedious journey was accomplished ;   130
And wisdom prevailed to stand before my lord,
So, though my tale be naught, I'll tell it out,
As clutching this sole comfort to my heart,
That man may suffer but what fate impart.
    CREON. What weighs thee down to such despondency ?
    GUARD. First set my own score clear, I did it not,
Nor saw who did. I'm not amenable.
    CREON. Why, the man picks covert like a master-
      bowman.
Come, sirrah, loose thy bolt.
    GUARD.   Dread gives me pause.
    CREON. Out and have ended it.
    GUARD.   I'll tell thee. One   140
Hath this hour past, strewn dusty earth, with more
Such funeral charity, upon the corpse
And vanished.
    CREON.   O the miscreant. Who was 't ? Speak !
    GUARD. I know not. Pick nor mattock there had delved.
The raw, unbruised soil was stark and printless
Nor shewed one scar to track the criminal.
But, when the day-guard first apprised and told us,
We were confounded ; for the corpse was hidden

Not as with regular entombment beneath ground,
But by such covering of filmy dust   150
As one might cast in pious houselling
Of an unburied body. Neither had dog
Nor any beast come nigh to it to touch it.
Then were hot words, as guard set blame on guard,
And like we seemed to fall to fisticuffs ;
For every man was guilty, not one proved.
All disclaimed knowledge ; and each was ready there
To handle molten metal, walk through fire,[8]
Or swear on God to attest his innocence ;
Till, all such inquest proving barren labour,   160
One spoke a word whereat we bowed us down
In utter terror, arguing, to wit,
That we must tell this thing and hide it not
From thine ear, O my king. His counsel won.
Lot cast the luck on me ; and I am here
Loathing no less to tell than thou to listen ;
'Tis a bitter errand to bear evil news.

   3RD ELDER. I marvel, good my lord, if this be not
Some act of God.
   CREON.   Have done with dotard's folly
Ere wrath consume thee. O, I know it well ;   170
There are who through the city wag their heads
And mutter in covert treason at my rule.
'Tis they have set men on to do this deed
For money. Money is the source and head [9]
Of all the world's misfortunes. Lordly cities
Money hath sacked, and driven men from homes,
And taught them felon ways and dismal crimes
And all ungodliness. But soon or late
This deed shall cost them dear. By which same token,
Find me the guilty, or by the God above us,   180
Death's self shall not suffice ; but ye shall hang
A living spectacle,[10] till all be told
And the knowledge mastered that ill-gotten gains
Bring more of sorrow than security.

GUARD. O yet one word, or must I, sir, be gone ?
CREON. Now, out upon thee for a saucy chatterling !
GUARD. But not the culprit.
CREON.   Culprit ? nay, what 's worse,
A hireling knave who'ld sell his soul for silver.
GUARD. O shame that fancy should so warp the
    judgement.
CREON. Fancy me no fancies. Find him, sirrah ;   190
Or find thyself in torment rue thine error.
                        [*Exit* CREON *into the palace.*]
GUARD. Praise to Almighty God ; my life is spared.
I hope again where hope I never dared.
                        [*Exit* GUARD *to right.*

A Pause.
3RD ELDER.
Full many a mystery this Earth doth yield,
    But none more marvellous than the child of Man ;
He knoweth year by year to plough the field
    And set the ox in span,
To net the fishes, snare the silly fowl,
    Track the wild creature to his mountain form,
Cross the hoar ocean, when the winds behowl   200
    The pathway of the storm.

4TH ELDER.
Speech and swift thought are his and cunning skill
    To flee the rainshaft and the frost's keen breath ;
All enemies, save one, bend to his will ;
    And that enemy is Death.
On good or evil will his fancies run ;
    The righteous soul hath honour in the land ;
The ungodly is outrooted ; such an one
    Never shall be my friend.

Enter the GUARD *leading* ANTIGONE.

1ST ELDER. O strange unenvious sight ! It is the maid
Antigone ; and on her hands are chains.   211
    ALL. The king ; call out the king.

Enter CREON *from door of palace.*

What is this clamour?

GUARD. My liege. I little thought to come again
Or face the terrible transport of thy wrath;
But our imaginings, by Fate belied,
Are turned to better. I have brought the culprit.
Nor was this mission by mere luck o' the dice
Thrust on me; mine alone 's the treasure-trove.
Take her and question her. Enough for me
That trouble 's overpast and I go free.   220
    CREON. Why hast thou taken her?
    GUARD.   She did the deed.
    CREON. And she of royal blood. Best give good heed
To what thou sayest.
    GUARD.   With these very eyes
I saw her pay him the last obsequies.
    CREON. How was she captured, fellow? Tell me all.
    GUARD. That will I, master. Thus it did befall.
We, when we passed from thy dread presence forth,
First scraped its covering from the clay-cold corpse
And left it bare and sat us down to watch,
Perched on a hill-top windward of the stench.   230
Then on a sudden, as the sun stood bright
At middle noon, and the heat was all a-shimmer,
There came a gust which blotted out the sky [11]
And filled the plain and marred its greenery
With whirling drift o' sand. We, muffled close,
Endured that plague of God; and, when it passed,
Behold this damsel crooning dolefully,
As when a mother bird returns and sees
Her empty nest and utters a shrill cry;
So she, when she beheld the naked corpse,   240
Raised wild lament and called a bitter curse
On its despoilers. Then with quick hands she wrought
To pile the thin dry dust and cover it;
And from a brazen stoup poured twice and again [12]

Libation on the dead. But we rushed down
And took our quarry, she no whit dismayed
But openly confessing all her guilt.
So was I glad and sorry at one time,
Sorry for her, glad for mine own escape,
Which is to me, as most men, the main matter.   250
    CREON. (*To* ANTIGONE.) Raise up thy head so lowly bowed to earth,
And answer for thine innocence.
    ANT.   I did it.
I am beyond denial.
    CREON. (*To* GUARD.) Go! thou art free.
(*To* Antigone.) Tell me—no parleying—didst know the order?
    ANT. I knew it. Marvel were if I did not.
    CREON. Yet hadst thou courage to transgress the law?
    ANT. The Almighty hath not set his seal thereon,
Nor spake kind Mercy for the piteous dead
In that fell utterance. Thy writ, O king,
Hath not such potence as will overweigh   260
The laws of God, not graven upon stone,
Immutable, which whence they are none knoweth,
Not of to-day nor yesterday, but fixed
From everlasting to eternity.
What, though man rage, I must obey that law,
And count it but a little thing to die,
For death must come; and, if I die to-day,
Why, I am glad to quit this world of tears.
Where is the bitterness? Far bitterer were 't
To leave my mother's son unsepulchred.   270
    1ST ELDER. The father's spirit in the child lives on,
Fronting misfortune with a soul of iron.
    CREON. Yet strongest iron, made brittle in the fire,
Will snap and shiver; and high-mettled steeds
Turn to the manage of a tiny bit.
Pride sorts not well with underling's degree,
Yet she is so puffed up that in offending

She glories at the front of her offence.
Unman me here, and man her in my stead,
If this shall go unchastened. Summon me forth   280
Her sister ; for the twain alike are guilty,
And the twain shall die. [*Exit attendant.*] Art shaméd
    for thy sin ?
    ANT. What shame to honour mine own kith and kin ?
    CREON. Was he not kin that died to save our home ?
    ANT. Aye, blood of my blood, and offspring of one
    womb.
    CREON. Then were thine act an outrage on his name.
    ANT. He would not say it, could he rise again.
    CREON. The one was noble, as the other base ;
Wouldst thou in honour give them equal place ?   289
    ANT. He was that brother's peer, not brother's slave ; [13]
And all mankind are one beyond the grave.
    CREON. In death foe still is foe, and friend is friend.
    ANT. Tis not in me thus to be cruel, but kind.
    CREON. Go, shew thy kindness then among the dead.
Woman must bow to man, when all is said.

Enter ISMENE.

    1ST ELDER. Look, where Ismene comes, her flushing
    brow
O'erclouded with presentiment of woe.
From lowering lids the storms are breaking now
And down fair cheeks the showers of sorrow flow.
    CREON. Treacherous viper, nurtured at my side   300
To suck my life-blood, when I knew it not :
Come answer for thy portion in this deed,
Or be for ever silent.
    ISM.   It was mine.
So she consent to it, I share her crime.
    ANT. 'Tis falsely said ; naught was betwixt us two.
    ISM. Yet side by side we'll brave the tempest through.
    ANT. The dead be my warrant how he found his tomb.
    ISM. Ah, let me share thy service, and thy doom.

ANT. Best not to meddle where thy hands are free;
My life will satisfy.
    ISM.   What's life to me?   310
ANT. Ask Creon here; for he hath all thy love.
ISM. Ah, mock me not; 'twill unavailing prove.
My life is bound in hers.
    CREON.   Her life is done.
ISM. Yet is she trysted to thy own dear son;
And wouldst thou slay his bride?
    CREON.   No bride for him
Whose heart is evil; others are to win.
ANT. O Haemon mine! hark to the bitter wrong![14]
CREON. This sweetheart prattle waxeth overlong.
1ST ELDER. Thou canst not part them; surely she is his.
CREON. Death comes between their wooing and their
    bliss.   320
1ST ELDER. Stands then the sentence that the maid must die
CREON. It stands; thou knowest it, as well as I.
Set them in ward. Give them but narrow room.
Henceforth we'll teach these womenfolk to keep their
home.[15]

The GUARD *leads* ISMENE *and* ANTIGONE *into the palace.*

1ST ELDER.
So sons must suffer, if a father stray;
    On children's children doth the curse descend;
Nor shall God's anger have been turned away
    Till it hath made an end;

As when the storm-blast on some jutting steep
    Vents its wild fury, and the tortured strand   330
Moans to the surf that from the sullen deep
    Rolls in the sable sand.

Thus on the honour of our ancient crown
    Are poured the vials of the wrath of God,
Till lingering hope, like a last star gone down,
    Is quenched in maiden's blood.

2ND ELDER.
Naught recks the Almighty of man's puny pride;
　His watchful eye shall slumber not nor sleep,
Who reigns in deathless majesty beside
　Olympus' dazzling steep,　　　　　　　　340

The mighty humbling from their high estate,
　The fool confounding in his vain device,
That man may learn to enter at the gate
　Of patient sacrifice.

' 'Twixt good and evil he shall not discern
　Whom God draws on to ruin ', saith the sage.
For, till the fire be kindled and he burn,
　He counts not Folly's wage.

Enter HAEMON.

1ST ELDER. Lo, yon comes Haemon, last-born of his
　　sire;
As lover weighed by leaden-hearted woe　　350
For the dead promise of his lost desire.
　CREON. What thought his bosom hides, we soon shall
　　know.
Is it in wrath thou comest, O my son,
For the doom delivered on thy late betrothed,
Or art content ?
　HAEMON.　　　Father, I am thine.
From thee I take my precept; nor would barter
Thy loving guidance for all the brides in Greece.
　CREON. 'Tis well, my child. Ever before aught else
Obey thy father. Wits should not go beggared,
Because a woman's fair; and he who takes　　360
A wanton wife to his bosom fondles ice.
So spurn her from thee. Let her go ungrieved
To find her luck of husbands with the dead.
Thus is it ever; loyal to country, loyal
To home; and the transgressor of the law,

Who thinks to come it proudly o'er his liege,
Him I esteem as nothing. Disobedience
Is the world's prime curse. It layeth towns in ruin,
Wasteth homes, dissolves in broken rout
Confederate hosts ; but all prosperity   370
Wherein salvation lieth for the most
Of men, is rooted in obedience.
Wherefore to froward woman let 's be stern ;
And, if we fall, why, we will fall like men,
By man's, not woman's mischief.
    1st Elder.   Truly said
If age trick not my judgement.
    Haem.   Good my father,
'Tis not my part to shew wherein thou errest ;
Yet may one counsel as well as doth another,
And I for thy behoof am vigilant
To mark the musings of the common crowd,   380
Which, standing in a muted awe of thee,
Dares not to speak its mind. There are mutterers
Darkly indignant for this maiden's fate,
Who say that woman was ne'er more abused
Nor gat worse wrong for doing of the right ;
For, thinking shame to leave her brother's corpse
A prey to savage dog or carrion fowl,
She merited, say they, a golden meed.
So runs the dark demur ; and, since to me
Thy safety is the dearest thing on earth,   390
I pray thee look to it. The wisest man
Scorns not betimes to learn humility.
When winter spates come tumbling from the hills,
The pliant sapling bends and bending lives ;
But the stiff tree-trunk, stubborn not to yield,
Goes hurtling down the flood. Stretch not thy sail
Too taut against the tempest ; else shall come
A buffet, so thy barque be overset.
    2nd Elder. This too is wisely spoken ; each hath
      right.

CREON. What ? by this stripling shall mine age be
schooled ?   400
Must I rule Thebes at other men's dictate ?
HAEM. Where one's all-powerful, 'tis no polity.[16]
CREON. I am the polity. Ye all are mine.
HAEM. Best monarch be then in a wilderness.
CREON. Misgotten son, so to affront thy sire !
Vile imp of mischief, minion to a wench,
Fate means her not for thine on this side death.
HAEM. Then let her die. and dying doom her friend.
CREON. No threats for me, sirrah.
HAEM.   Is it a threat
To answer folly with the voice of truth ?   410
CREON. Now, by yon Holy Mount, I'll brook no taunts,[17]
Or thou shalt smart for it. Go fetch her forth
That she may die before her lover's gaze.
HAEM. Vain thought ! I shall not see't, nor thou
behold
Thy son again. Go, vent thy coward spite
On such as truckle to a tyrant's might.

> [*Exit* HAEMON *to right.*]

3RD ELDER. My lord, his youth is hot and impetuous.
CREON. Let be ; he's welcome to the braggart talk.
He shall not save the damsels.
4TH ELDER.   What, wilt slay
Both sisters ?
CREON.   Nay, thou art right. I'll pardon her   420
Whose hands are clean. But for that other one—
There is a rocky cavern, desolate
And wild, where never foot of man hath trod ;
I will immure her there, with provender
No more than to avert the State's pollution.[18]
And there at her instant cry the God of Death
She so reveres, shall haply come to save her,
Or there she'll learn when it is passing late
They spend but barren labour who the dead placate.

> [*Exit* CREON *to palace.*]

3RD ELDER.
O sovereign Love, to turn man's wealth to woe,   430
    Vanquish the mighty or enthrall the weak ;
Still for blind mortals shall thy watch-fires glow
    On maiden's blushing cheek.

Thy spirit ranges o'er the ocean flood ;
    It finds a dwelling where the wild goats stray ;
So none may flee thee, be he deathless God
    Or mortal of a day.

4TH ELDER.
On whomsoe'er thy witching spell be cast,
    His crazy wits go wandering. At thy call
The very saint shall tremble ; for at the last   440
    Love lures him to his fall.

In the warm glances of the bashful bride
    Love shines imperious. Through the fleeting hours
Unconquerable he sits, enthroned beside
    The everlasting powers.

Enter from the palace ANTIGONE, *bound in shackles and
accompanied by two guards.*

  1ST ELDER. Strength fails me to withhold the welling
    tear
Or hide my guilty thought. For now, alas,
I see the innocent maiden fare
On that last bridal way, where all must pass.

  ANTIGONE. O sirs, my countrymen, behold a maid 45c
On her last travel faring, where the sun
Shall never more illume the dismal shade ;
But, ere my course be run,
Death take me living to his chill embrace.
No bridal melody for me is sung,
Nor bridal garland wreath'd ;
Yet in a space
Shall I and the Lord of the Dark Night be one.
  2459   H

2ND ELDER. And yet the wide world over shall be
  breath'd
The legend of thy glorious fate.   460
No wasting sickness unallieved
Nor battle at the foeman's gate
Shall work thy doom,
But, self-arraigned, inviolate,
Thou shalt pass living to the awful tomb.

  ANT. O water-springs of Dircé, sacred ground
Of Thebes, whose many chariots roll to war,
Hark to the loveless voices and the sound
That mocks me from afar.
How strange my lot, who in that craggy tomb   470
Forlorn must languish, not, as others are,
Or dead or living still ;
Since is no room
For me on earth nor yet beyond the bar.

  3RD ELDER. Ah rash, presumptuous maid, thou didst
  not well
To hold Law's majesty so light,
Or in thy foolish pride rebel
Against the immeasurable might
Of Justice' throne.
Yet haply thou dost here requite   480
Thy father's sin in suffering for thine own.

  ANT. Mine is no mourner-throng nor bridal strain
Of happy choir. For me the blessed light of day
Shall never shine again ;
But I must pass unfriended down the pilgrim way.

Enter CREON.

Peace ! For if weeping or wailing would suffice
To stay the hand of death, who'ld ever cease ?
Convey her hence ; and in the vaulted tomb
Enfold her. There in solitary sojourn
Let her abide to perish or to live,   490
As list she may ; our hands shall have no stain.

Ant. O bridal bower, whose narrow prison-house
Is my eternal sepulchre, beyond
Thy portal the Lady of the Twilight waits
To give me welcome, and that lost company
Who were my friends ; myself the last in time
To perish and of all most miserable.
They will be glad to see me ; father glad,
And mother glad, and glad my own dear brother,
For whom I wrought to lay his body fair   500
And do on it the sacraments of death,
Aye, and for whose fond sake am come to win
This guerdon.
What have I done to overstep God's law ?
And how should I cry Him mercy at my need,
Or look to Him for grace ? For all my prayers
Are mocked ; and to my piety men give
Another name, as though 'twere sin. If such
Be Heaven's will, I'll know it, when I'm dead.
If not, O may the like on them be visited.   51c

   1st Elder. Wild words betray the tempest of her
    soul.

   Creon. (*To the* Guards.) Make speed, an ye would
    keep your carcass whole.

   Ant. O, the shadow of death lies in that utterance.

   Creon. Aye, doom now waits on no uncertain chance.

   Ant. Farewell, dear land of Thebes, farewell !
Look down, ye princes, on my sore distress.
The cruel summons sounds my knell,
My captors round me press.
I die, because I loved too well
The ways of holiness.   520
               [Antigone *is led away*.]

3rd Elder.
    So once fair Danaê, immured [19]
      Within her brazen room.
    The darkness of the night endured
      And the silence of the tomb.

Yet was she honoured with more high renown
   Than other women were ;
For God's own self in shower of gold came down
   To visit her.

Fate calls ; and who shall save ?
   Not wealth nor battled tower,   530
Nor ships that traffic over the far wave
   Help at that hour.

4TH ELDER.
   Others of old were found
     Who suffered like to thee.
His children savage Phineus bound [20]
     In bonds of misery ;
And, where betwixt the Narrows' misty door [21]
     The dark-blue waters wind,
Yearlong in dungeon deep they bore
     The anguish of the blind.   540

For royal house or lineage rare
     Shall nought avail,
When the Shadowy Sisters hover near, [22]
     And told is the tale.

Enter the blind prophet, TEIRESIAS, *led by a boy.* [23]

TEIRESIAS. One pair of eyes must serve for two, my
    masters,
When blind men walk abroad.
   CREON.   How now, Teiresias ?
   TEIR. Ill news, my lord, ill news.
   CREON.   Why, what 's amiss ?
   TEIR. On fate's nice edge thy fortune tottereth
To ruin's verge.
   CREON.   God's mercy on us. Speak.
   TEIR. List to an old man's warning ; and be wise. 550
I sat in the augur's seat, where the fowls o' the air [24]
Make daily muster. There I heard a cry,
Not as is wont, but frantic hurly-burly

Of weird, outlandish voices. With red claws
They tore each at the other savagely,
And their wings made music of no doubtful presage.
Then gat I straight in fear to the high altar ;
But when the fire was lit, it gutted out ;
And from the ash trickled a clammy ooze
Did reek and sputter. Like a bursted bubble, 560
The gall gave forth, and the unlarded bones [25]
Lay bare ;—which signs my acolyte reported,
Who, as I guide others, doth the like for me ;
So knew I of the sacrifice refused
And tokens unvouchsafed. (*Pointing at* CREON.) Thou
 art the cause ;
'Tis thy ways have brought our city to this pass.
For the altars are polluted ; bird and dog
Snatch the offal from yon mouldering carcass
Of Oedipus' dead son, and strow it wide.
Therefore are the Gods in high displeasure 570
To taste no flame of offering nor receive
Our litanies. Therefore is the birds' song
A senseless gibber ; which have gorged their full
On the fat of dead man's meat. Then, O my son,
Be prudent. All men err ; but, whoso erreth,
May yet in timely wisdom mend his ways.
Blind pride bewrays the fool. So heed me now,
And sheathe thy sword over a fallen foe.
 CREON. Is't so, sir prophet ? am I to be the butt
Of every covetous knave ? I'm parcelled out, 580
Sold at a price for traitor's merchandize ;
And now would the very seers make game of me.
I know you all. Go, traffic at your lust—
Alloys of Sardis, yellow gold from Ind ; [26]
But this man's burial ye shall not procure,
Aye, though the eagles of Almighty Zeus,
Should lift yon carrion to the topmost skies,
And lay it at the throne. Marry, I would laugh
To see the gross abomination done—

Well knowing mortal can defile not God—²⁷ 590
Ere I would yield his bones a sepulchre.
  Teir. Unwise, unwise; and Wisdom beyond price.
  Creon. And Folly, mark me this, the beggar's vice.
  Teir. To such a vice art partial then thyself.
  Creon. Bah, probe in a prophet, and discover—pelf.
  Teir. Another word and the dark truth will out.
  Creon. Who cares how dark, so gain be not its root?
  Teir. Small gain to thee, ere yet the day be done.
  Creon. No marketing my resolve!
  Teir.   Hear then. O foolish one.
Not many courses of the Sun's swift steed 600
Are thine to witness, ere one of thine own seed
Shall render life for life, and doom for doom.
Since thou hast sent souls living to the tomb,
And those whose portion was in holy field,
Left desecrate, disfavoured, unaneled,
Wherefore do demons, watchful as the ghoul
Athirst for blood, lay wait upon thy soul;
And nigh the place where the foul deed is done,
Weeping and wailing shall be heard anon.
In every city where the dogs have mauled 610
Shreds of that carcass, shall thy curse be called.
Such doom I utter thee in righteous wrath
Since thou this day hast dared to cross my path.
Boy, lead me hence; and let him learn in pain
To walk more humbly and his tongue refrain.
                              [*Exit* Teiresias.]
  1st Elder. Dark words, King Creon, and grim pro-
      phecy;
Nor, since my gray hairs came, knew I the seer to lie.
  Creon. O 'tis a fearful thing to break my pride;
And yet—and yet, to see my life destroyed. 619
  2nd Elder. Be wise, while yet there's time.
  Creon.   What should I do?
  2nd Elder. Unprison her and give him burial. Go.
  Creon. And think ye that?

3RD ELDER.   Aye, linger not afield.
CREON. O fate is hard to wrestle with—I yield.
4TH ELDER. Up, and away then. Leave it to none else.
CREON. An axe! give me an axe! and since I'm false
To mine own word, I'll loose where I have bound.
God's law is best; or where is salvation found?
                             [*Exit* CREON.]

1ST ELDER.
   O son of the Lord of heaven, whom men hail [28]
     By myriad titles at their hour of need,
   Indwelling Power of Thebê's watery vale,   630
     Whence sprang the Dragon's seed;
   Oft, where the Nymphs their fairy revels hold,
     Thou hast been seen aloft the Cloven Mount,[29]
   What time the cressets star the hills with gold
     Beside Castalia's fount.

2ND ELDER.
   Look on the city which thy soul doth love,
     Succour her children in their time of dearth.
   Come quickly from thy mountain home above,
     Or cross the sounding firth.
   Lord of the muster of the stars of night,   640
     Lighting thy mystic chorus as it sings,
   Come, Dionysus, when the dawn is white,
     With healing on thy wings.

       After a pause, enter the GUARD.
Call not man's life, ye neighbours of our king,
A steadfast matter. Fortune setteth up;
And Fortune putteth down; and all our ways
Are compassèd about with mystery.
Creon was great and glorious in his day,
Saviour of Thebes, sole monarch of her throne,
Blest with a noble seed—and all is lost.   650
He lives; yet would I count the like of him
But as a stalking spectre. Men grow rich.
They get them pride of power and kingly state;

But, be life's joy once vanished, I'ld not give
For all such circumstance one wreath of smoke.
   1st Elder. What heavy news dost bear for the king's
house ?
   Guard. Dead, dead—and dead by doing of the live.
   1st Elder. Who is the fallen ? Speak ; and whose the
hand ?
   Guard. Haemon is gone. He wrought it.
   2nd Elder.   Father or son ?
   Guard. In wrath he lifted up his hand and spoiled 660
His own life's treasure.
   2nd Elder.   Ah, the seer saw true.
But from the house who comes ? Tis Creon's queen
Euridicê. Have tidings reached her ear ? 30

Enter Euridice.

   Eur. O my people, as I went to pray,
I heard a cry which smote upon my heart
And left me swooning in a sore amaze.
What is it ? Tell me true. I am not strange
To sorrow.
   Guard.   Hearken, O lady. Truth is best.
We came, the royal master and thy servant,
To the plain's verge where lay the mangled corpse 670
Of Polyneices. There we laved the dead,
And o'er his relic lit the funeral fire
Of branches green fr' th' tree, set earth upon 't,
Then turned our footsteps where the maid was held
Within the hollow chamber of the rock.
Near as we drew, from that unhallowed bower
Issued a wild, strong cry ; whereat the king
Bitterly sighed and said, ' Out and alas,
My weird is come ; and the way I'm wending now
Is of all the woefulest that man may go. 680
'Tis my son's voice ; go quickly, bring me word
If it be he or am I mocked of God.'
Then at his bidding peered we through the gap

Rent in the rock's rude masonry, and saw
The maid aloft, slung by a slender weed [31]
Around her neck ; and that young man was there
His arms flung close about her ; and his tears
Flowed fast in ceaseless lamentation
For his father's folly and for his own lost love.
Then cried the king, ' What ails thee, O my son ?   690
What pain-wrought madness hath so marred thy wits ?
Leave her. Come forth ; O I entreat thee, come.'
But with strange eyes he glared upon his sire,
Spat out on him, yet never a word spake he,
As from his thigh he drew the hilted sword.
The aim went wide. The father fled. And then
In self-abhorrence he leaned on the sword's point
And through his bosom drave it to the haft.
In failing arms he took and clasped the maid
Close, close, while life yet lingered, and the gush   700
Of crimson blood dewed all her pallid cheek.
There lie they in each other's arms, and he
Hath won his bride, not here
But on the further shore.—All for to prove
How much unblest are the wild ways of love.
                                    [*Exit* EURIDICÈ.]
    1ST ELDER. The queen is gone, and not a word let fall
Whether to bless or ban. 'Tis strange.
    GUARD.   Aye, strange ;
And yet belike within she'ld nurse her sorrow
Not blazon it before the vulgar gaze.
    1ST ELDER. My heart misgives me yet. The sullen
        silence   710
Of a broken heart bodes worse than frantic grief.
    GUARD. Then I'll within to learn what mystery
Dwells in her dark intent. [*Exit* GUARD *into the palace.*]

    Enter CREON, *following* HAEMON's *body on a bier.*
    3RD ELDER. The king ; and close before him comes a
        train,

Whose secret grim no shroud can hide,
Of his great pride
The fruit and aftermath of pain.
   CREON. Two souls are here, by sorrow made at one,
Father who, lost in murderous counsels, slew,
And murdered son,   720
Cut off, before his youth's blithe course was run.
I little knew,
As now I know, the sum
Of all my folly. Surely it was God
Who my small store of wisdom overthrew
And down into the dust my happy fortunes trod.

Re-enter GUARD.

Thy garner, sire, is full. Thou bringest store
Fresh from the field; and in thy home is more.
   CREON. What, worse and worse, my friend?
   GUARD.   Thy queen is gone.
The mother—weep for her—is as the son.   730
She stood before the altar. Passed a knife.
Thick darkness veiled her eyes. And ended life.
Yet in that last moment, with her dying breath,
She cursed the man who did her son to death.
   CREON. Death hath no mercy. Pray we never so,
All must pass timely to his haven dark.
Now one, now two,
Are stolen from me, as the swift hours go.
'Tis bitter work;
And had I not enow   740
Of misery? With this my double sorrow
Life were all misery. God save the mark,
May life for me be ended, ere it dawn to-morrow.
Come lead me hence, to mine own ruin fain,
Where'er I set my hand, all runs agley.
Wife have I slain
And son. Fate hath been very hard to me this day.
                    [*Exeunt* CREON *and* GUARD.]

1st Elder.

    Faileth not happiness
      Where men be wise.
    Such shall win fullest bliss
      Under the skies.   750

    Toward the great powers above
      See thou walk lowly.
    None the Immortals love
      Saving the holy.

    Vain word and frantic boast
      God will chastise,
    And such shall win sorrow most
      Under the skies.

                [*Exeunt* Chorus.]

MEDEA

DRAMATIS PERSONAE

CREON, King of Corinth.
JASON, betrothed to his daughter.
MEDEA, wife of Jason.
Two children of Medea.

Their Nurse.
Their guardian-slave.
Messenger.
Chorus of Corinthian women.

The scene is laid before the house of JASON *in Corinth, the
home in which he has settled after his mission to Colchis,
and to which he has brought* MEDEA, *the foreign princess
who had there helped him by her sorceries through the
perils attendant on the seizure of the Golden Fleece.
From the central doorway issues an aged Nurse in
sorrow.*

NURSE. O, never, never should the Argo's barque
Have winged her passage 'twixt the Azure Straits ¹
Faring to Colchis, nor the woodman's axe
Ravaged the pine-glades on Thessalian hills
To furnish forth the ocean-rovers' quest
After the Golden Fleece. For never then
Had Love beguiled my mistress for to quit
Her native castle by the Black Sea shore
And follow Jason, till in Corinth here
She came to dwell with him, fond, foolish wife,   10
Yielding a woman's one most costly treasure,
Her soul's fidelity.—But now all 's changed.
The chord is snapped between them, Jason turns
To wiving ; and a right royal bride is his,
Daughter of Creon, Corinth's overlord.
And Medea, ah, poor lady, how she raves,
Broken vows and dishonoured troth lamenting,
Till the Gods grow weary of her tale of wrong.
No food she'll take, but lies abandoning
Her soul to utter sorrow ; nor stirs at all,   20

But wasted and wan with weeping, prints her cheek
On the cold ground, and harks no more to comfort
Than ocean crag or the billow shoreward rolling.
Whiles she will turn her pallid neck and mourn
Half-musingly for that which she has lost,
Her home, her father, all she once held dear,
Yet once betrayed for this same Jason's sake.
Her very children are an abhorrence to her;
No smile she gives them; and I quake for fear
Of her dark purpose. Dour she is of spirit,   30
Terrible in wrath; and, if she make a foe,
It must go hard with them that use her so.
[*Enter* Jason's *two children with their attendant guardian.*]
Lo, yonder come her children fresh from play,
Poor innocent babes to care oblivious.

GUARDIAN. What? lingering here, old beldame, still
          content
To croon thy selfish sorrows and neglect
Thy lady mistress in the lonely hall.

NURSE. Fie, ancient warden of Jason's little ones,
What loyal slave but shares a liege's sorrow?
'Twas melancholy brought me to unburden here   40
My soul's oppression, and to tell the winds
How my dear mistress suffers.

GUARDIAN.   Ah the poor crazed dame—
Saving her reverence—more 's the need for tears,[2]
For little recks she of the last blow fallen.

NURSE. What 's that, old man? Say on.

GUARD.   Nay, 'tis no matter.

NURSE. Hide it not, prithee, from thy fellow gossip;
My tongue can keep its secret.

GUARD.   This much then.
I heard a body say—though they marked me not—
'Twas by yon fountain where the gaffers sit
A-playing at the draughts [3]—I heard one say   50
That the king is purposed—look 'ee idle chatter,
As like as not; God grant it may be so—

Well, one was saying that the king is purposed
To pass on Medea and her children with her
Decrees of banishment.
    NURSE. Then we are lost; for ere one storm be
      weathered
Its fellow bursts upon us. O my babes,
What 's he that was your father? Curse him? Nay,
That must not be; for he 's my master still.
Yet to his own folk is he a traitor sealed.   60
Go, children, get you in. Let them not nigh
Their mother's black displeasure; I have seen her;
There 's that writ in her eye which bodes small good
To such as cross her purpose. Heaven send
A foe it be to suffer, not a friend.
    MEDEA (*within the palace*). Woe 's me! Woe 's me!
    NURSE. 'Tis she. In, children, in! nor cross her path;
Fierce burns her spirit in its stubborn wrath.
    MED. O woe! O misery! O spiteful fate!
Truth is turned traitor. Hope is desperate.
Then why prolong this world-abhorréd breath?   70
End, end, life's agony; and welcome death.
    NURSE. In, tarry not. The storm-clouds gather fast,
Till passion kindle to a withering blast.
                [*The children go within.*]
    MED. O spiteful fate! O misery! O woe!
What weddéd wife was e'er abuséd so?
Begone, ye accurséd! Ruin seize the home
Confounding children in a father's doom!

    Enter a chorus of four Corinthian women.
  IST WOMAN.
        Loud the lamentation
          Echoes on the wind.
        Broken heart lies bleeding   80
          For a fate unkind.
        Sounds of tears confound the ears;
          Tears the vision blind.

2ND WOMAN.
>Dark her spirit labours
>>To some dismal end.
>Desperate grief beyond relief
>>What shall it portend ?
>Yet, stranger of the broken heart,
>>I will be thy friend.

MED.
Come, thou dread stroke of Zeus, from Heaven fall. 90
Cut the thin thread of life, and end it all.

3RD WOMAN.
>Hark, what prayer is lifted
>>Soothest sleep to crave,
>Sleep without a waking,
>>Sleep beyond the grave.
>Yet God on high shall hear her cry
>>And he is strong to save.

4TH WOMAN.
>Over the dark ocean
>>Came she from afar,
>Through the fretting frith she came,   100
>>Past the foaming bar,
>Learning late the woful fate
>>Of a wanderer.

MEDEA *comes out of the central door.*

MED. O women of Corinth, I would not have it
That for a stubborn churl ye should upbraid me,
Because I keep my house and bear withal
A proud demeanour. Therefore am I come forth.
Full well I know that 'tis a stranger's part
To suit her manners to the land she dwells in ;
Sour faces make few friends.[4] Yet now the blow   110
Of swift misfortune hath utterly undone me.
Life's joys are fled away ; and I fain would die.
For he that was my all, my own dear husband,

Is become a monster to me. Verily
Of all things living that draw mortal breath
We women are the most distressful creatures,
Who, first, with a multitude of worldly goods
Must buy us husbands, lords over limb and life ;
Running herein great hazard of freak chance ;
For, to new home and habit unfamiliar,   120
The young bride needs must use diviner's art
To gauge untutored the temper of her mate.
Be he indulgent and the twain harmonious,
Life is all bliss ; but, falls it otherwise.
Far better 'twere to die. For a man hath vantage
Who may betake him, when the home-life palls,
To mate with cronies and in companionship
Beguile his humour. But for us poor wives
'Tis solitary communion with the one same soul
For ever. O 'tis said that, while men fight,   130
We women lead a safe snug life at home,
Comparison most false ; rather I'ld stand
Three times in the battle-front than once bear child.⁵
But you and I—how different is our case ;
Home is yours, life's joy, and friends to love.
I am alone, an outcast, rapt away
From mine own people, here to be cast aside
And by false lover spurnéd. Naught have I,
Mother none nor brother none nor kinsmen,
To shield me from the storm.   140
Yet this sole boon, no great one, would I crave :
If that a way be found to punish Jason
And his bride and him that did bestow the bride,
Be secret.—Tim'rous and fearful is a woman,
Frail help when the battle 's joined and bare 's the steel.
Yet touch but once the honour of her bed,
And none shall take a bloodier revenge.

   1ST WOMAN. Lady, 'tis granted ; for I pity thee
And own thy quarrel just.

   [CREON *the king is seen approaching from the right.*]

But yonder, see,
The king approaches, with tidings for thine ear. 150
   CREON. Away, thou sour-faced, sullen-tempered
    shrew,
Out of the land, I say ; no dallying.
Here I am master ; and, till thou art gone
Beyond the limits of my realm's domain,
I will not set foot home.
   MED.   O misery !
O cruel, O fatal blow ! what have I done
To suffer thus ?
   CREON.   'Tis no time for mincing phrases ;
I am afraid of thee. Thy jealous temper,
Thy skill in magic arts, thy muttered threats
Which late have reached my ear, point all one way, 160
Bidding me tremble for my daughter's life.
Better affront thee straightly here and now
Than smart to-morrow for to-day's indulgence.
   MED. Alack, alack, my name is my undoing
Now, as ever ; the name that I have gotten me
For subtle lore. Yet 'tis a baseless slander.
I am not learnéd much. I think no harm
To thee and thine, O king. Thou wrong'st me not.
Tis he, 'tis Jason wrongs me. Marry thy child
To whom thou wilt ; but let me bide in peace. 170
   CREON. Soft words, soft words ; but the dread is in my
    heart.
Forth thou shalt go. No argument can touch me.
   MED. For mercy, king, I kneel. Thou hast not heart
To thrust me forth.
   CREON.   Such words are wasted breath.
   MED. O God, see mine oppressor ! [*She clasps his knees.*]
   CREON.   Woman, unhand me.
Must I call the guards ?
   MED.   Nay, nay, I will submit.
Exile is nothing ; but this one brief day
Suffer me to tarry for my children's sake,

2459   K

And furnish them a refuge. For myself
I have no thought. But pity, O pity them.　　　180
　　CREON. Mine is no tyrant temper ; oft and oft
Humanity hath been my mischief. Yet
For this one day stay on, if stay thou must ;
For that this should work me harm is out of question.
But, if to-morrow's morn discover thee
Still lingering here, then thou shalt die the death.
That is my word fixed and immutable.
　　　　　　　　　　　　　　　[Exit CREON.]
　　CHORUS. Alas, poor lady, whither shalt thou turn
By ceaseless surge of troubles overborne ?
　　MED. O the world 's awry ; that 's certain. But think
　　　not　　　　　　　　　　　　　　　　　　190
The play is all played out. Yet there remains
For them that marry and that give in marriage
An ordeal to the uttermost. What ? Should I thus
Have cringed and fawned, yea, so much as touched his robe
Except to cozen him ? But he, poor fool,
Has plumbed the depth of folly, suffering me
Here to abide one day, in the which, God helping,
I shall lay him and his child and Jason dead.
O many are the ways of death I know ;
Yet know not which to use ; whether to burn　　　200
The house about them or with stealthy sword
To broach the bridal chamber ; or, best of all,
The quick way and the way in which I'm skilled,[6]
With magic drug to quell them.—Aye, but then,
They dead, what home, what sanctuary for me ?
There is none. So will I wait a little while
And if appeareth some strong tower of refuge,
Well—but, if not, I'll take the sword in hand
And screwing tight my courage slay the twain,
E'en though I die for it. O Hecaté,　　　　　210
Awful mistress of dark worlds below,[7]
Whose hand is with me and whose shrine I serve,
Assist me now. Up, up, Medea, shrink not.

Now comes the touch of valour. Summon thy skill
And on to the dread emprise. Ponder thy woes,
Nor suffer more the mockery of thy foes.

CHORUS.

1ST WOMAN. Now babbling brooks flow backward ;
   Now Truth is turned to lies.
  Now man is false and froward ;
   And Faith forsakes the skies. 22c
  But woman is strong to vanquish wrong
   And how shall man despise ?

2ND WOMAN. Minstrels of ancient story
   Have hymned of our deceit ;
  Yet answer made we never
  For that Phoebus the Song-giver
  Hath left us skilless ever
   In the art of music sweet.
  But herein have we a token
  That hereafter shall be spoken 23c
  The full tale of pledges broken,
   Where man and maiden meet.

3RD WOMAN. O lightly she deserted
   The land where she was born,
  Travelling to a strange land,
   Lonely and forlorn,
  Here but to win the world's disdain,
   And a false lover's scorn.

4TH WOMAN. Lo, honour's bond is loosened,
   And vows dissolve in air, 240
  For the links of love are riven,
  And the home whence she is driven
  To another hath been given
   And a new queen reigneth there.
  But forsaken by her lover
  She shall wander the world over,
  And no haven shall discover
   In the dark night of despair.

Enter JASON.

JAS. 'Tis pity, woman, that for a rash word's sake
Thy right to dwell in peace is forfeit thee.   250
Hot temper is great bane.—Yet I'll forgive ;
And such provision as is mine to offer
Against the needs of exile, count it thine.
MED. O damnéd villain,—words do fail my tongue
To express thy craven manhood—darest thou come
To look on me ? Dare, say I ? 'Tis no daring,
But brazen impudence that brings thee here.
And yet 'tis well ; for holding commune with thee
I shall both ease my gall and wound thee home.
From our first meeting let the tale be told.   260
Life I gave thee—all can vouch for it
Who sailed the good ship Argo—when thou cam'st
To set in yoke the flame-flew'd bulls and sow [8]
With death the teaming acre. That old serpent,
Whose sleepless coils encased the Golden Fleece,
I slew, and raised for thee a beacon-light
Of sure salvation. Home and father then
I did forswear to cross the seas with thee,
More fickle-fond than wise. For all of which
I now am betrayed and treacherously supplanted   270
By this new charmer. O hand of mine that oft
Was clasped in his, O lips that he hath kissed,
Vain, vain your pledges, promise turned to dust—
Yet soft ; I'll speak him fair as friend to friend
That he may show the baser. Tell me, prithee,
Where should I turn me ? To father ? or to kin,
That for thy sake I quitted ? Foes they are
That one time were my friends ; and for that exchange
I have won, good lack, the envy of the world.
O mine 's a precious pattern of a husband,   280
Who'ld ruin the woman rescued him from death,
And a pretty tale he'll have to tell his mistress,
That his wife and bairns are beggars. Mighty God,
Why hast thou given us tokens manifest

Whereby to sift the sterling and the counterfeit
Of precious metals ; but in man hast set
No stamp or visible sign to mark the rogue ?
   1st Woman. Sore disputation past all remedy,
When lovers fall to quarrelling.
   Jas.   It would seem
That I must not bate my powers of eloquence,   290
But like a skeely mariner take in
My sail and run close-reefed before the blast
Of thy shrill utterance. Thou pilest high
The imagined debt of favours past. But I
Would set all down to the compelling power
Of sex. Thou lovedst, and loving could not else
But bend to the strong yoke of passion
And save thy darling's life. Am I for that
Beholden ? 'Twas some service ; that I grant ;
But balance against it the benefits returned.   300
Thou wast from savage Barbary transferred
To Greece, where men know equity and law ;
Didst win, too, wide renown for thy great wisdom,
Not at the world's end continuing obscure.
And now this royal marriage, for the which
Thou dost reproach me, what is it but clear gain
To thee and thine ? Nay, let me speak ; for, mark,
Well knowing how the poor man finds few friends,
I did bethink me of this excellent counsel
To wed a monarch's daughter, that my house   310
Should suffer lack no longer, but, uniting
Two families in one, we should continue
In prosperous abundance. Was it ill devised ?
Thyself thou couldst not say so, were it not
That our disunion hips thee. Women count
Wedlock to be the summit of life's joy ;
But, be their privilege one jot curtailed,
The jades' affections veer like weather-cocks.
Better for man if children had been born
Some other wise than by the female kind ;   320

For woman is the source of all our plagues.

1st Woman. Jason is apt meseems to trick out argument;
Yet to my judging he hath done grievous wrong.

Med. Come not to me with plausible profession :
One word shall silence thee. Tis proof of guilt
That doing wrongly thou didst secretly,
Hiding from me thy purpose. As for riches,
I esteem them not, nor prosperity so won ;
For the smart outdoes the pleasure.

Jas.   Wait awhile
And thou'lt confess thine error.

Med.   Bravely done   330
To cast me the woes of exile in the teeth.

Jas. It was thy choice, not mine ; blame 't not on me.
Yet am I ready with unstinting hand
To minister to thy necessities.
Speak but the word ; and I will give thee tokens
That my friends entreat thee well.

Med.   Friends, money, nay,
All that thou hast to offer, keep it thine.
I'll not lay finger to it.

Jas.   God in heaven,
Witness my offices so kindly tendered,
And (more 's the woe to her) so rudely scorned !   340

Med. Go thy ways ; thou'rt itching to be gone
And end this dalliance from thy darling's lap.
Go, wive ; and, when the wiving's done, ah then
God knows thou'lt wish thyself unwived again.

[*Exit* Jason.]

Enter Messenger.

Chorus. Lo, here a servant comes all travel-worn,
As sped with news out of some distant land.

Mess. Lady, I have great tidings for thy comfort.
Aegeus, King of Athens, Pandion's son 9
Hath heard of thy late tragical misfortunes ;
And for that the tale is bruited everywhere   350
How thou art knowledgeable in curious arts,

And hast great skill in medicine, he would have thee
To minister to his distempered age.
Therefore, when thou art driven forth from Corinth,
He bids thee welcome and in Athens town
Proffers thee shelter and safe sanctuary.
   MED. Is't so ? Then God reward him boundlessly
For his unbounded kindness ; and such leech-craft
As my poor wisdom masters, I do place
At his most honoured service. Yet I tremble   360
Lest, having taken me, he should repent
And at the bidding of mine enemies
Should yield me up again. What is my surety ?
   MESS. He will not fail thee—
   MED.   His oath is pledged upon it ?
   MESS. Sworn is he to stand by thee to the end.
   MED. Enough ; 'tis well ; and on the path of victory
My feet are set. Hope dawns, and where the night
Was darkest, salvation hath appeared.
Go, fellow, call back Jason to my sight. [*Exit* MESSENGER.]
I'll speak him fair, tell him I am content,   370
Beg him to keep my children here a space—
Not meaning to betray them to the foe,
But that through them I may effect my wiles.
A faery robe and a coronet of gold
I'll send as dower-gifts by my children's hands
To Jason's bride ; and, if she put them on—
With such fell sorceries I will infect them—
'Tis cruel death to her and to all who touch her.
And then, alas for the sequel ! I will slay
My own dear children ; and utterly confounding   380
The whole house of Jason I will quit the land.
Awful is the deed ; but I must do it.
I'll not be mocked. No man shall call me tame,
Or soft or spiritless—far otherwise :
A faithful friend, but a most fatal foe ;
For their fame is greatest who do bear them so.
But soft, not a word of this to Jason.   [*Exit* MEDEA.]

1st Woman.

  O sons of Athens, heavenly blest,[10]
  Bright children of the sky.
  Your land no evil shall molest,[11]   390
  Nor enemy come nigh ;
  But through an air as crystal clear
  Ye foot it lightsomely.

2nd Woman.

  There erst the holy Muses nine
  Did golden Harmony bear.[12]
  There springs by Aphrodite's shrine
  Cephisus flowing fair ; [13]
  Whence she doth use to fill her cruse
  And scent the fragrant air.

3rd Woman.

  With rosebud garland sweetly twined 400
  About each golden tress,
  The goddess moves amid her Loves,
  That mate with Kindliness.
  And how shall such company accord
  With this, a murderess ?

Re-enter Jason *and* Medea *with gifts.*

Jas. At thy behest I turned me. What new thing
Wouldst thou require of me ? Woman, say on.
 Med. Jason, forget my words. Forgive my folly.
I have repented and bitterly have chid me ;
Fool, said I, what ingratitude is this   410
That, when my husband plans for my behoof
To marry a king's daughter and to raise up seed
For brothers to my babes, I bear't amiss ?
Who am I to cavil when the Gods are kind ?
My helpless, friendless children, must I not
Consider their well-being ? Such was my thought ;
And it was borne on me how that thy act
Was good, and mine insensate folly. Stay !
Children, children, come hither from the house

And kiss your father and be friends with him,   420
As I am. All is peace between us now. [*Re-enter children.*]
Go, kiss his hand. (*Aside.*) Ah me, the pity of it !
Those darling arms so lovingly outstretched
Shall in a while be still.

    JASON. Lady, thine altered purpose I applaud.
'Tis a wise woman's act. And you, my children,
What anxious thought your father has bestowed
For his babes' welfare. Maybe that even now
Ye shall live on in Corinth. Bless you both !
'Tis my unceasing prayer that I may yet   430
Behold you grown to hale and lusty youth,
Triumphing ever above your enemies.
(*Turning to* MEDEA.) What 's this ? Blanched cheek, wet
    eyes and head averse.
Have I said ought, woman, to make thee sad ?

    MED. 'Tis nothing ; my thoughts were with these little
    ones.

    JAS. Take heart ; I'll see to them.
    MED.   O, I do believe it.
But a frail thing is woman, born to tears.

    JAS. Why so heavy-hearted for the children ?

    MED. I was their mother ; and, as I heard thee wish
Long life to them, a pang shot through my heart   440
Lest they should die.—'Tis past ; and for myself,
Who am obnoxious to the royal house,
I freely acknowledge banishment were best.
But for these, I prithee, supplicate the king
That they remain under thy fostering care.

    JAS. Whether I shall prevail I cannot tell ;
But yet will try.

    MED.   Set on thy bride to ask.

    JAS. It may be she might move him.
    MED.   That she will,
If she 's a woman.—And lo ! I'll lend thee aid.
Gifts I will send her, costly beyond compare,   450
A faery robe and a coronet of gold,

And the children here shall bear them. Blest indeed,
A thousandfold more blest than other women
Shall be that noble dame, with thee for husband,
And with a robe to wear, which long ago
The Sun, my glorious ancestor, bequeathed
An heirloom to his line. Come, little ones,
Take the dower-gifts and to the happy bride
Convey them straightway. Such they are, I ween,
As she shall not despise. And, when ye enter   460
The door of the rich palace, make your prayer
To escape the banishment, and therewithal
Proffer the ornaments ; and—mark you this—
Into her own hands place them, her own hands.
Now get you gone at once, and speed you well.
Glad be the tidings you return to tell.[14]

   [*Exeunt the children, their* GUARDIAN *and* JASON.]
 1ST WOMAN.

   Doom hovers o'er the victim's head :
    Hope's withered at a breath.
   Fate beckons the unwitting maid
    To take the enchanted wreath ;   47c
   And round her golden brow is laid
    The coronal of death.

 2ND WOMAN.

   O bright is the robe with a faery bloom,
    Where magic lustres play ;
   Nor recks she of the hidden doom,
    To set her in array.
   But in the dim heart of the tomb
    Shall be her wedding day.

 3RD WOMAN.

   O woe 's the bride who in her joy
    Is parted from her lord ;   480
   And woe 's the price that he must pay
    Who broke his trysted word ;
   But woe for those most who must to-day
    Die by their mother's sword !

Re-enter GUARDIAN *with children.*

GUARDIAN. Mistress, they are pardoned. The decree
  of exile
For them is disannulled. With a good grace
The lady took the gifts ; and all is peace.

MEDEA. Ah me !

GUARD. Why dost thou stand so plunged in melancholy ?
My words should make thee glad.

MED.   O woe is me !   490

GUARD. This happy news and thy receiving of it
Are at strange odds.

MED.   And yet again, woe's me !

GUARD. What have I said amiss ?

MED.   No blame to thee.
What thou hast told, is told. Yet tears must flow
For all the evil that this heart doth know.

GUARD. Nay, pluck up courage. Home thou yet shalt
  come.

MED. I shall bring others to a long, long home.[15]

GUARD. 'Tis a common lot to part with children dear ;
And what fate sends us, mortal man must bear.

MED. I'll bear, as best I may. Go, get thee in   500
And let the children's needs be duly seen. [*Exit* GUARDIAN.]
O children mine, yours is a home and a city,
In the which ye shall live on, for ever
Motherless, while I must wander far, alone,
An exile. Never shall these eyes behold you
Grown to your full estate ; never this hand raise
The bridal torch to light your happy marriage.
Out on my rebel pride, was it for this
I bred you ? Was it for this that I endured
The strong pangs of child-birth ? Ah, poor fool,   510
What dreams I had that you would keep me
In my old age, and in my death would lay me
Tenderly to sleep—and the sweet dream is gone,
Is gone. Ah me, why gaze you on me so ?
And smile that smile never to be smiled

Again ? O, at the look of those glad faces
My heart melts, I cannot do it. Farewell
My old resolve. I'll take them with me. Why,
To give him pain, should I myself have double ?
It costs too dear ; and so, resolve, farewell!   520
And yet—to falter here and be to them
A laughing-stock ! O that must never be.
I'll dare, and charge it on my coward heart
To conceive such craven things. Go, children, on.
Enter before me. None may participate
In my great sacrifice, or the blood be
On his head. My hand shall not flinch—— [*She pauses.*]
Hold, hold, cruel heart. O spare these little ones.
They yet shall be thy joy in the far land
Where thou art going. Nay, nay, by the fiends of hell 530
It shall not be for my enemies to mock them.
There can be no escape. E'en at this hour
The crown is on her brow ; in that robe of death
The bride is perishing ; and I must tread
The path of misery, they tread it too.
One last farewell. Come, children, give your mother
A hand to kiss. Dear hand, dear head, dear face,
Dear beyond utt'rance. Loved ones, fare ye well,
But in another world ; this world is yours
No more—his deed, not mine.—O sweet embrace,   540
Warm cheek and tender breath. Begone, begone ;
I dare not look on you. The pain unhearts me.
Yet in my soul doth such strong passion move
As shall o'erride all argument of love. [*The children enter.*]
Lo, yonder comes a messenger in haste,
And the foam is on his lips. What news ? What news ?
   Mess. O dreadful deed ! Fly hence, Medea, fly !
   Med. Why should I fly ?
   Mess.   The royal maid is dead,
And her father with her ; and it is surely
Thy sorceries have done it.
   Med.   Praise the day !   550

MESS. What ? Art thou mad to rejoice at the report
Of this unhallowed murder ?

MED.   Be not wroth.
Tell me what way they died ; and doubly welcome
Shall be thy tale, if they died horribly.

MESS. All was blithe and merry in the palace-halls
When the children came with Jason. For the tale
Went round the feud betwixt the two of you
Was ended. So we servants thronged about,
To kiss their hands and their pretty curls ; and I,
For the very lightness of my heart, went through   560
With them to the bride's chamber. There she sat,
And her eye was fain for Jason, seeing not
The children ; but, when she saw them, she grew pale
And hid her eyes and turned her face away
In dudgeon. Then her husband stayed her wrath,
And spake her soothingly, ' Nay, frown not, sweetheart ;
They have my love and sure they shall have thine.
Accept their gifts ; and go, beseech thy father
To remove the ban of exile, for my sake.'
Then, seeing the finery, her heart was won,   570
And Jason's word found favour in her sight.
Nor were he and the children but an instant gone
When she arose and took the spangled garb
And put it on and set the golden crown
About her forehead, atrimming of the curls
In a bright mirror, so she did laugh to see [16]
The inanimate reflection's mimic show.
She left the chair. She paced the palace hall
With dainty mincing tread, ever and anon
Stiffening the ankle of her lily foot   580
To feast her gaze on th' gown. And then, O horror !
She blenched, trembled from head to foot, reeled back
And swooned athwart the chair. One grey-haired dame
Fancied some frenzy fit of heaven's sending
Was come on her ; ' Bless thee,' she cried [17] ; and then
She saw the white foam frothing at the lips,

She saw the staring eyeballs upward strained ;
She saw the pale, pale face ; and her benediction
Turned in that moment to an eldritch shriek.
This way ran one of us to tell the king ;   590
To summon back the bridegroom went another,
Till the palace hall was loud with hurrying feet.
But, in the brief while that a swift runner
Would pace a furlong, the unhappy maid
Recovered herself up ; sight came again ;
Her tongue was loosened and she groaned. Ah me !
What twin affliction there made war upon her.
The golden diadem about her brow
Flamed forth devouring fire. The lissom robe
Ate her white flesh, poor maid, poor martyred maid. 600
She started from the chair, one sheet of flame,
Tossing her head now this way and now that
To dash the crown from off it ; but the gold
Clung fast ; and ever as she shook, the fire
Blazed out the hotter ; till she sank at last
Forspent with agony. Such was she then
That her own father scarce should know his child.
Dim were th' eye-sockets, the fair features blurred ;
From head dripped blood and fire ; and off the bones
The flesh distilled, as liquid resin oozes   610
From a pine, while underneath the venom gnawed
With jaws invisible—a thing of horror ;
Nor was there one of us did dare to touch it ;
For we were schooled by fear. But the old father
Unwitting of all this came suddenly
And stumbling on the body raised a cry
Exceeding bitter, and folded her to arms,
Kissed her, and said, ' Poor lass, what unseen power
Hath wrought this havoc on thy innocent life,
To snatch thee from me, and bring me to the grave   620
A lone unchilded man. O let me die
With thee, my child, my child.' But, when he ceased
And sought to raise his aged frame from earth,

Lo, he and she were joined past severance,
As ivy to a bay. Then sore he wrestled
To brace him up upon his knees, but she
Clung close to him, and, as he toiled amain,
He tore his withered body flesh from bone;
Till he too wearied and, resigned to a fate
He could not master, yielded up the ghost.   630
There side by side lie child and father dead,
And no tears of ours can ever bring them back.
Thy part I pass in silence. Look to thyself
When the hour of reckoning comes. O Vanity,
The life of man is but a shadow, and all
His wisdom foolishness. None, none is happy;
One than another may come better off
As touching fortune. But happy? no, not one.
                              [*Exit* MESSENGER.]
   1ST WOMAN. Sore punishment is fallen and shall fall
On Jason, ere this day be past and over.   640
God's will be done; yet O for the fate of her
Sent down to death for that she married him!
   MED. Friends, I must do the deed, ere I go hence.
For, whilst I tarry, crueller hands will slay;
And so, since die they must, myself will do it,
The mother who gave them life.
Come, heart, put on thy steel. Out, sword; and on,
Medea, to where life's sad goal stands beck'ning.
Flinch not. Remember not how they are dear.
But this brief day forget thy motherhood.   650
There's time for tears hereafter.
                    [*Exit* MEDEA *into the house.*]
   1ST WOMAN.
     Sun, darkly shroud thy sober ray;
       No kindly lustre lend.
     Be quench'd, thou blesséd light of day,
       Before this dismal end.
     Skies, in this hour put forth your power
       To stay the murderous fiend.

2ND WOMAN.

> O a child born is labour lost,
> And a mother's care vain,
> When passion doth not count the cost   660
> To punish pain with pain.
> But she takes the life she loveth most
> And the blood she sheds is her own.

1ST CHILD (*within*). O save me, save me, save me ; or I die.

2ND CHILD. No help, no help, my brother ; lost are we.

1ST WOMAN. Hark to that cry, the death-cry of a child.

2ND WOMAN. Who'll dare within, ere yet their blood be spilled ?

1ST CHILD. O succour, for God's sake ! The time is short.

2ND CHILD. All, all is over. The sword is at my throat.

1ST WOMAN. O stern as adamant, heartless as craggy stone,   670
To slay with thine own hand the offspring of thy womb.

3RD WOMAN.

> In the long chronicles of time
> They tell of but one like thee,
> Who in the frenzy of her crime
> Brought doom on souls of three ;
> For her babes to drown she flung her down
> And perished in the sea.[18]

4TH WOMAN.

> O never was a heart won
> Nor ever a maid wed,
> But sorrow seals the bliss begun   680
> When the light of love is fled ;
> Yet the foulest sin is white and clean
> Beside this awful deed.

Enter JASON.

JASON. Tell me, women, is Medea yet within ?
Or is she fled from hence ? Much need she hath

To hide her deep in the bowels of the earth
Or to take wing to the wide sky's abyss.
Yet not for her, think it not, is my concern ;
But for my children. I am come to save them,
Lest on their persons vengeance should be ta'en   690
For what their mother's done.

    1st Woman. The great God help thee, Jason ; knowest
      thou not
What trouble is upon thee—thus to speak ?

    Jason. What ? Does she plot also to take my life ?

The doors of the palace open, revealing Medea *and the*
bodies of her two children.[19]

    Medea. Thy pains are wasted. Look ! yet hast thou
      ought
To say, say on. [Jason *draws his sword, as though to attack*
                       her.]
               Down, felon sword.[19] [*At a sign from*
    Medea *the sword falls from his hand to the ground.*]
                         No power
Is thine to touch me ; by the wizard charm
Of the Sun, my ancestor, I am immune
From thine ineffectual violence ; and his chariot
In a breath shall waft me whither I would be.   700

    Jas. Demon accurst, in the sight of God and man,
Was it for this I brought thee out of Barbary ;
And gave my heart to a traitor ? Woe 's the day
When heaven sent thee to me as a fiend
To dog my footsteps !—no woman, but a beast,
A serpent such as lurks in cruel caves
Beside the Tuscan sea. Hell take thy soul,
For an inhuman mother and unnatural wife !
Alas for the bride I never shall know more ;
Alas for my lost little ones !

    Med.   'Twas not thy fate   710
To mock me, Jason, nor to know life's joy,
When thy great wrong was done. What should I care
For thy reviling ?—Call me beast or serpent

Bred in cruel caves beside the Tuscan sea ;
It is enough for me to wound thy soul.
  Jas. Thy soul is wounded too no less than mine.
  Med. The pain is welcome, so that pain be thine.
  Jas. A strange, strange mother, children, yours hath
    been.
  Med. Children, ye suffer for a father's sin.   719
  Jas. 'Twas not my hand that brought you to your doom.
  Med. They arē no more ; that truth shall touch thee
    home.
  Jas. Their avenging sprites shall haunt thee to the tomb.
Yet one last boon I'ld beg, and that is all ;
Grant me their bodies for the burial.
  Med. Nay, to my hand shall that last service fall.
Their grave I'll dig, then take me to the soil
Where the noble Aegeus, Athens' king, doth rule.
Go, get thee gone and bury thine own bride.
  Jas. I go, of children reft, of wife betrayed.
Once let me kiss them, ere I leave them here.   730
  Med. As well go supplicate the empty air.
  Jas. Heaven visit vengeance on her guilty head,
Who thus would part me from my own dear dead.
               [Exit Jason. *The palace doors close.]*
  1st Woman.
        What Fate ordains, man cannot change;
          Man's purpose Fate denies.
        The path of Providence is strange ;
          All dark the future lies.
        Yet these have trod the ways of God,
          And the ways of God are wise.[20]
                   [Exeunt Chorus.]*

NOTES

AGAMEMNON

1. The ancient Greeks used three dice.

2. A proverbial saying, based on the name given to night 'the kindly one'. The Greeks often gave friendly names to gods or objects that they dreaded, with the idea of placating them. Thus the stormy Black Sea was called the 'Euxine' or 'Hospitable'.

3. Chains of beacons were used for signalling during the Persian invasion of 480 B.C. This speech, though not written till 458, may therefore be in some sense a 'topical allusion'. Ida was the mountain above Troy ; Lemnos an island in the Aegean ; Athos a headland on one of the three jutting peninsulas near Salonika ; Makistos a mountain in Euboea ; Euripus the strait between Euboea and the mainland ; Asopus a river near Thebes : after that the message passed by stages over the Saronic Gulf (between Attica and the Peloponnese) and arrived at Mount Arachnaeus above Argos itself.

4. They did not observe, that is, the customary ceremony of a triumphal banquet.

5. Respect for the holy buildings of a conquered country was one of the chief points of international etiquette.

6. Scamander, a river of Troy. Apollo had, in his wrath, sent plague into the Greek camp.

7. Here, as frequently throughout the ensuing scenes, Aeschylus makes use of what is called 'tragic irony'. That is to say, he puts into the mouth of Clytamnestra words apparently innocent to those with whom she is conversing, but bearing a more sinister meaning to the audience, who know what is in her mind.

8. The arrival of Agamemnon so soon after the fire-message from Troy constitutes one of the chief difficulties in the plot of the play. Certainly the 'unity of time' is here strained to an almost intolerable degree ; and Professor Verrall has propounded a brand-new theory to explain it. He thinks that the beacon was in reality a ruse of Clytamnestra, intended primarily as a signal to her friends in Argos which should announce to them the arrival of Agamemnon, and warn them to be ready to stand by her in case of need. Her explanation to the Chorus is, according to this theory, a lie from beginning to end—a suggestion which surely destroys the poetry of the whole passage at a blow. There is, in fact, no call for so heroic a solution. The Greeks well understood the convention by which a considerable passage of time was expressed by a ten minutes' chorus. To them it was almost equivalent to a 'curtain' ; moreover a little knowledge of stage production will make clear that such incongruities, so glaring to the author or producer, are very easily swallowed by an interested audience.

9. The Greeks, especially if sailors, dated their seasons very much by

the stars. The period between the rising of the Pleiads (May) and the setting of the Pleiads (November) was considered the only safe time for sea voyages.

10. Tragic irony. Clytamnestra entangled Agamemnon in a net before she slew him.

11. 'Methinks the lady doth protest too much.'

12. Clytamnestra was daughter of Leda, the mother of Castor and Pollux.

13. The Greeks always despised Orientals' luxury—their divans, cushions, carpets, and so forth.

14. Tragic irony again.

15. The swallow was often used as a similitude for unintelligible foreign speech. Aristophanes mentions the 'swallow-talk' of a politician suspected of being an 'alien'.

16. Cassandra, Priam's daughter, was loved by Apollo and by him endowed with the gift of prophecy. When she rejected his suit, he added the curse that nobody should ever believe her. So her warnings of the fate which was coming upon Troy had passed unheeded.

17. Scylla, the monstrosity half woman, half fish, with writhing snake-like heads, lay on the Italian side of the straits of Messana, opposite the whirlpool Charybdis. From her cave above the sea she stretched out her necks and picked sailors off passing vessels—a fate which befell some of Odysseus' crew. Probably the legend was partly a reminiscence of a pirates' stronghold, partly an imaginative adaptation of the octopus.

18. The mystic number three was always associated with the dead. Compare on *Antigone*, line 244. In saying farewell to the dead body the words were, for instance, three times repeated.

19. Aegisthus, the guilty lover and fellow-conspirator of Clytamnestra, does in the actual play appear at her side and hold a somewhat heated dialogue with the Chorus. His appearance, however, adds little to the play.

20. As Professor Murray has suggested, Clytamnestra does really seem to act like one 'possessed'; and to feel that the spirit of revenge, incarnate in her, was alone responsible for the murderous act.

21. In the subsequent plays of the Trilogy, the *Choephori* and the *Eumenides*, Orestes plays a leading part, hence the name of the Oresteia is given to the whole series. In the *Choephori* he returns a grown man to Argos, and slays Clytamnestra and Aegisthus. In the *Eumenides*, or *Furies*, he is pursued by avenging spirits, and only escapes by taking sanctuary at Athens, where the goddess appoints the famous 'court of the Areopagus' to do justice between him and his pursuers, and where he is accordingly tried and acquitted.

22. This chorus ending is, in point of fact, taken from another part of the play. I am guilty of having treated Aeschylus' ending in a very cavalier fashion, it is true; but then it must be remembered that the end of the *Agamemnon* was only the beginning of the *Choephori*.

ANTIGONE

1. The main interest of the play depends upon the enormous importance which the ancients attached to burial. It was the duty of the living to provide for the comforts of the departed ; to this end they would periodically offer food and drink at the tomb for the convenience of the ghostly occupant. One lady is related to have sacrificed large quantities of clothing because one of her relatives reported in a dream that the nether world was chilly. The superstition, however, insisted above all on decent entombment ; a soul whose body had not been properly buried was liable to exclusion even from Hades. A mere handful of dust, however, was sufficient to satisfy the superstitious demand.

2. Dircê, in point of fact, is on the wrong side of Thebes for the sunrise. But atlases were rare in Greece, and Sophocles may well have been in error.

3. The warriors of Argos carried a white shield.

4. Cadmus, visiting the site of Thebes, found a dragon there and slew it. Advised by Athena to bury its teeth, he obeyed, and armed men grew from the soil. They fought each other and were for the most part slain ; but the survivors became the ancestors of the Theban race.

5. The expedition of the ' Seven Princes against Thebes ' was made the subject of one of Aeschylus' surviving plays.

6. Bacchus or Dionysus, god of the revel and mystic rites, and the special divinity of Thebes.

7. The royal house of Thebes may be thus tabulated :

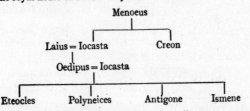

8. Little is known of the Greek use of ordeals, to all appearance curiously akin to mediaeval English customs.

9. Creon is right. The Greeks were an avaricious nation ; and there was scarcely a city in which traitors could not easily be bought.

10. Such punishment is more oriental than Greek, a sign perhaps of Creon's growing pride and violence of temper.

11. Greece is a very dry land with few rivers and no meadows to speak of. Dust storms are therefore a not unnatural phenomenon.

12. See on *Agamemnon*, note 18.

13. Implying that, though free men would all be equal in Hades, slaves would still be inferiors.

14. Haemon's character introduces a love element, singularly rare in Greek drama. Its rarity is one of the most striking differences between ancient and modern literature—and moreover an interesting commentary on the position of women in ancient times. Chivalry was an unknown ideal.

15. Women were expected neither to be heard nor seen in Greek towns. The decent housewife remained in the seclusion of her home, almost as closely as a Turkish lady of to-day.

16. There speaks the democrat—who in Athens of course was very much to the fore.

17. Mount Olympus—though scarcely visible from Thebes.

18. Creon several times shows a conventional desire to escape from ceremonial pollution, cp. below, line 591; Antigone is to be provided for at first—and after that left to her fate. Much in the same way the Spartans starved one of their kings to death, walling him up in a temple, but removing him just before he died. Compare also the punishment of vestal virgins who proved unfaithful to their vows.

19. Danaê, daughter of Acrisius, king of Argos, was walled up in a brazen tower, because an oracle had foretold that she would give birth to a son who would slay his grandfather. Zeus, however, visited her in the likeness of a shower of gold (an idealization of bribery ?) ; and she gave birth to Perseus, who duly lived up to the prophecy.

20. Phineus, a Thracian king, blinded and imprisoned his children on account of the false accusation of their step-mother.

21. The allusion in the Greek is to the ' Symplegades ' or 'Clashers', the two ' dark blue ' rocks which, according to legend, stood at the mouth of the Black Sea, and which were supposed to 'clash' together and entrap passing vessels. Were there once icebergs in the Black Sea which might have given rise to the myth ?

22. The Fates, three in number : Clotho, who spun the thread of a man's life ; Lachesis, who assigned it to him ; Atropos, who cut it short at the appointed place.

23. Teiresias, the Nathan of Thebes, to whom had fallen already the unpleasant duty of revealing his sin to Oedipus.

24. The observation of birds was a favourite form of augury among the ancients ; cp. the omen of a flight of birds which attended the foundation of Rome by Romulus.

25. In a normal sacrifice it was not customary to burn the whole victim (a holocaust) ; certain parts were picked out and, in particular, the thigh bones were wrapped up in fat taken from some other portion of the carcass.

26. 'Electron', a silver-gold brought from the mines of Mount Tmolus, which lay south of Sardis in Lydia.

27. Does Creon wish to tone down his impious remark ? or is it Sophocles' own conscience ? At any rate the pious poet is not specially successful at depicting blasphemy.

28. Dionysus, the god of revel, &c., whose cult had sprung up in many Aegean countries and who was known by various names among various peoples. He was the god in whose honour the dramatic festival was held in the theatre.

29. The ridge lying above Delphi and below the crest of Mount

Parnassus, between which flows down the Castalian spring through a narrow cleft or fissure in the rock. These spots were usually associated with the presence of Apollo and the Muses rather than Dionysus and his revel-band. The firth mentioned below is the Euripus, flowing between Euboea and the mainland.

30. The introduction of Euridicê seems almost superfluous, even for the purpose of killing her off later to complete Creon's cup of bitterness. But doubtless it is necessary that there should be some one on the stage for the Guard to address ; and Euridicê's silent exit on receipt of the news might be very effective in action.

31. Hanging was the favourite form of suicide in Greece ; it was never, I think, used as a punishment.

MEDEA

1. The Greek alludes to the 'Symplegades', see *Antigone*, note 21. For the details of the story of the Argonauts see note 8.

2. There are many realistic touches in the character of the ' Guardian '. The Greek word is ' Pedagogue ', or ' child-leader ', a slave employed to watch over the children and take them to and from school.

3. Draughts were a common pastime with the Greeks. A vase-painting shews Greek warriors playing draughts at Troy.

4. The Greeks were an extremely sociable people and looked askance at anyone who did not make friends or go out for conversation in the market-place. Women, however, were usually expected to remain more quietly at home. The fact is that Euripides is depicting in Medea something more than the wronged wife. Her character is partly a study of an alien set among a foreign and unsympathetic population, partly of a clever personality who finds it difficult to suffer fools gladly and who thereby wins the reputation of exclusiveness. Euripides himself knew something of this trouble. His face in extant portraits gives the impression of an embittered man. We may be sure that he felt some fellow-feeling with Medea's loneliness.

5. An often-quoted line, which shows Euripides' genuine endeavour to enter into the mind and feeling of a woman. For a Greek, indeed, it is an amazing piece of imaginative insight, when we remember the contempt in which women were normally held.

6. Medea, it must be remembered, was a witch—and was regarded by her fellow-citizens with something of the aversion which usually attends such superstition. On the voyage from Colchis she had persuaded the daughters of Pelias (Jason's uncle, who had sent him on the quest of the Golden Fleece) that they could restore their father's youth by cutting him up and boiling him in a cauldron. The experiment was not a success ; and Jason and Medea were forced to flee the land of Iolcus in Thessaly where Pelias had been king.

7. Hecate, the mysterious goddess of the lower world, sometimes identified with Artemis and the Moon-goddess. She patronized witchcraft, was worshipped at the cross-roads, and fed on the blood of murdered persons.

8. Jason was sent by his uncle Pelias to obtain the Golden Fleece, which was kept at Colchis on the Black Sea under the guardianship of a dragon. Jason sailed with some comrades in the ship Argo. When he reached Colchis, the King Aeëtes promised him the fleece if he would yoke two fire-breathing oxen, and plough a field and sow therein the remainder of the dragon's teeth not used by Cadmus at Thebes (see *Antigone*, note 4). Medea, Aeëtes' daughter, fell in love with Jason, and by her arts enabled him to resist the fiery breath of the bulls and to send the guardian dragon to sleep. The fleece was captured, and Medea sailed away with Jason. ' Flame-flewed ' should strictly mean ' with chaps or gullets of flame '— such a concoction is not, however, unlike the words which Greek poets coined ; and I can find no better.

9. In the original play Aegeus himself arrives on the scene, having been to Delphi to consult the oracle and met with little success there. The dialogue in which Medea offers her services and Aegeus promises her sanctuary is somewhat tedious.

10. This chorus is a tactful and beautiful compliment to the Athenian audience.

11. The Athenians believed their ancestors to have been the aboriginal inhabitants of Attica. The country had by this account been exempt from the invasion of migratory tribes and was in this sense inviolate. But the epithet was strangely inappropriate in the year 431, when the *Medea* was produced ; in that year the war against Sparta began ; and every spring thereafter came an enemy army, which systematically ravaged the countryside.

12. Harmonia, the mother of the Muses.

13. Cephisus, one of the streams, hardly worthy of the name of river, which flow through the plain of Athens.

14. Tragic irony (see *Agamemnon*, note 7).

15. Again tragic irony. Note how the Chorus here are let into the secret, though their tongues are tied rather by dramatic convention than by their promise. In the *Agamemnon* the Chorus are far more a part of the play and are there really mystified by Cassandra's dark hints.

16. The ancients used bronze mirrors, highly polished.

17. The Greeks believed a fit to be a visitation of Pan or of some god, and regarded it as a sign of divine favour.

18. The reference is to Ino, daughter of Cadmus, who, having by her marriage with Athamas incurred the anger of the Gods, threw herself and her children into the sea.

19. In the original play Medea probably appeared on the roof of the palace in her winged chariot and well out of Jason's reach. Such a contrivance being awkward upon a modern stage, I have inserted the line in which Jason's sword is dashed by magic from his hand.

20. This somewhat trite passage of proverbial wisdom was a tag used by Euripides at the conclusion of several of his plays. Perhaps the applause drowned its obvious platitudes.

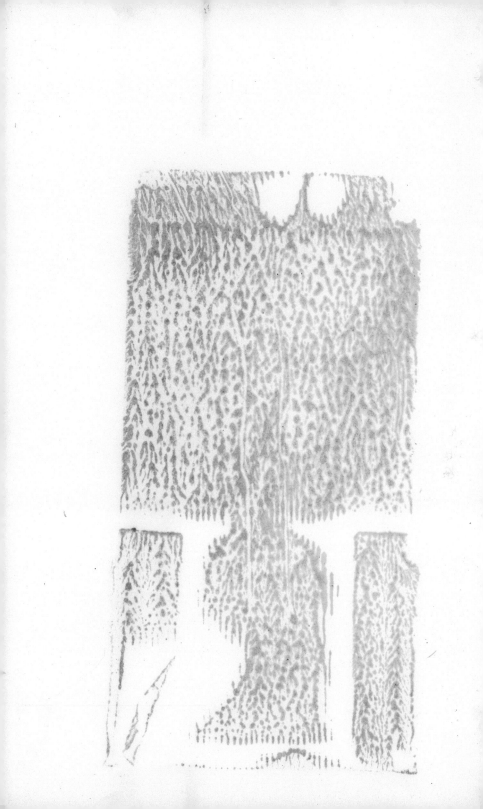